# Wings
*of a*
# Hero

●

# Wings
## *of a*
# Hero

*Canadian Pioneer Flying Ace*
*Wilfrid Wop May*

●

Sheila Reid

Vanwell Publishing Limited
St. Catharines, Ontario

Sheila Reid wishes to acknowledge the generous cooperation and assistance of Denny May, who provided much of the material, and the May family for their input.

First published in Canada by Vanwell Publishing Limited, St. Catharines, Ontario

Reprinted in 2005

Design: Linda L. Moroz-Irvine

Vanwell Publishing Limited

1 Northrup Crescent
Box 2131
St. Catharines, Ontario  L2R 7S2
Canada


Printed in Canada

Photo Credits: All photographs courtesy of the May Family Collection.
Cover: Wop May, 1930; inset, Wop May 1928

Canadian Cataloguing in Publication Data
Reid, Sheila, 1938-
    Wings of a hero : Canadian pioneer flying ace Wilfrid Wop May

Includes index.
ISBN 1-55125-034-9

1. May, Wilfrid Reid, 1896-1952.  2. Bush pilots - Canada,
Northern - Biography.  3. Air pilots, Military - Canada -
Biography. I. Title.


TL540.M388R45 1997       387.7'092       C97-931142-X

*For Wop*

From Edmonton's rough, dusty streets came a lad
    Who had high dreams of flying one day.
He enlisted to serve in the first World War
    As a Flying Corps pilot — Wop May.
Got a DFC Medal to pin on his chest,
    And a fortunate chance to retire,
When he spiralled the dashing Red Knight off is back
    With his skill and Roy Brown's cannon fire.

Fogs prowled, and blizzards howled
    And raging tempests blew,
But brave Wop May endured them all
    As ever on he flew.
A bold mechanic by his side,
    He dared to take a chance,
And through uncharted northern skies,
    He flew by the seat of his pants.

In the soul-stirring dawn of mechanical flight,
    When persistence and pluck proved their worth,
A volley of daring bush pilots took off
    To open up Canada's North.
Among'em Wop May made a name for himself
    As he ferried both men and supplies
From his base at McMurray to Simpson and on
    To Aklavik's cold boreal skies.

Near McPherson, the last of the year '31
    Albert Johnson ignited a fray:
In a craze he shot Constable King in the chest,
    And to spot him, Eames called in Wop May.
Wop flew his Bellanca along Johnson's tracks;
    Kept police on the Mad Trapper's trail,
And when Johnson was found on the Eagle's cold bed
    The dark lid on his coffin was nailed.

From Edmonton's rough dusty streets came a lad
    With a bold dream that opened the way
For the age of air transport in Canada's North —
    The courageous bush pilot, Wop May.

"Wop May" Lyrics by Bob McQuarrie, music by Bill Gilday, with permission from The Gumboots

About the Author

Sheila Reid was born in Hamilton, Ontario, and raised all along the CN's Transcontinental line. She graduated from the University of Manitoba and taught in Winnipeg schools until 1993, when she began her writing career. She has written several children's books, plays, newspaper columns, and commentaries for CBC Radio. She and her husband live on a prairie farm in Manitoba near the Red River.

Sheila grew up seeing Wop May as a familiar face in her grandmother's scrapbook. She didn't know much about airplanes and flying, however, until she began researching and writing this book.

# Contents

# Errata

*Please note these changes to the text.*

Page 7   The May family came west in 1902

Page 9   Date on photo should read 1911

Page 14   Date on photo should read 1918

Page 14   Paragraph 2, "he headed West into the Sun." While this is not possible at 11 am, the term "heading west" was used to refer back to the Allied lines.

Page 14   Last paragraph should read: "So, down Wop dodged and dived, three thousand feet, until..."

Page 18   The log book (on page 15) did not mention "Guns were jammed," though they were.

Page 22   King George V (not King George VI)

Page 25   Photo caption: "Wop May with Curtiss JN-4. The name was on top so it could be seen when he was flying the aircraft upside down."

Page 26   Photo caption: "Wop May in flying gear with Curtiss JN-4 'Jenny'. Photo was taken at the Calgary Exhibition, 1924."

Page 27   Photo caption:  "Wop May in Ryan Standard J1, Edmonton, 1924." This aricraft was a modification of the Curtiss JN-4 'Jenny' and was owned by J. Harry Adair of Lake Saskatoon, Alberta.

Page 48   Paragraph 2, sentence 1 should read: "On June 21, 1979, a commemorative flight was organized by Les Stahlke, Executive Director/Pastor Pilot with the Lutheran Association of Missionaries and Pilots."

Page 48   Paragraph 2, sentence 2 should read: "The sons of the two flyers, Denny May and Bob Horner, shared in flying the re-enactment with Les Stahlke and Russ Janzen of the Edmonton Flying Club, in the open cockpit of the 1930 Fleet "Finch" which was shined up for the occasion."

Page 50   Date should read 1929

Page 51   Date should read 1929

Page 100   Replace "July 7, 1919, Air Mechanic Licence #1" with "December 15, 1931, Air Engineers Certificate #A726."

Page 102   Medals/Honours list

| | |
|---|---|
| DFC, 21, 100 | Medal of Freedom, 91 |
| Great War Medal, 22 | OBE, 101 |
| McKee Trophy, 101 | Victory Medal, 22 |

*I would also like to add my thanks to the following, who were inadvertently left out of my foreword:*
Tahoe and Dr. Lincoln Washburn of Bellevue WA, who flew into the NWT with Wop May in 1938;
Wil Penner of Steinbach, MB for proofreading, sub-titles and producing the index;
Vera Lickert, my aunt, for keeping an album of clippings for the family;
Joanna Rowan, my stepdaughter, for her promotion and support;
Tracy Rowan, my stepdaughter, for her enthusiasm and promotion of the book;
Dr. Douglas Faulder, aviation historian from Edmonton, for his attention to detail;
Alan Bennett of Grimsby, ON for his attention to detail and additional information in his book *The Last Flight of the Red Baron*.

Denny R. May
Edmonton

# Foreword by Denny May

**Wop May** is a hero to many. But when he died in June of 1952 he was just "Daddy" to me. Our relationship, like many fathers and sons', had become tenuous – I was a teenager with my needs; he was a tired man with his. We were working it out. It has only been with the passage of time that my father has become a hero to me. The more I learn, read, and talk to people, the more I have come to understand what a great man he really was. That he was kind, generous, physically tough, a great teacher, a wonderful shot with a rifle (even with one eye), and a really good pilot. He was, in the eyes of some, super-human, which may account for the many myths that persist about him. For example, a lady in Peace River told me she had her first airplane ride with Wop May in 1897! He would have been not quite a year old in that year.

As I got into the research for this book I realized again how much I didn't know about him. I regret that I did not ask him the questions for which I now need the answers. Some of the answers I have found from other people, but some questions will go unanswered, forever. One of the motivations that got me started on this research in the first place was to correct the many errors that have appeared in other books, magazines, and newspapers over the years. To find out for myself just who Wop May really was, and to share that with others. This book is as accurate as Sheila and I can make it.

In reading through his correspondence, and in remembering what he told me as a kid, there are two discoveries in particular I would like to share...

I asked him one time why he had not kept a log book past the first few weeks of W.W.I. He told me that he, like many others, did not believe they would survive another flight into battle, so what was the point. How sad for all of us, for a log book of those experiences would have helped us understand that part of our history.

The other one had to do with his unshakeable faith. He spoke of it first in a letter to my sister Joyce: "What I'm trying to say is that God controls everything." He spoke of it to me during that fateful trip we took together in 1952. Although I didn't realize it at the time, it would be one of the last things he would say to me: "Don't be sad when I die. It's fate. When my time is up, I will die."

Many, many people have helped us with this book. I'd particularly like to thank the following, many of whom are now gone.

Family members: Vera Fife (Wop's sister), Derek Lickert (my cousin), Joyce May (my sister in Australia), Vi May (my mother), David May (my son), and my wife Margaret;

Family friends: Kay Dunlop (Edmonton) for filling in many details, and Gladys and Walter Hill from Fort McMurray;

Doctors Malcolm Bow and Harold Hamman (who were involved in the 1929 Mercy Flight);

Bush Pilots "Punch" Dickins and Stan McMillan;

Pilot Mark Heiderman (who provided a flight in a biplane for Sheila and me);

Bob Horner (Vic Horner's son);

Rev. Les Stahlke, Lutheran Association of Missionaries and Pilots (LAMP);

Bill Welsh, Manager, Edmonton Flying Club;

Russ Janzen, Manager of the Edmonton Flying Club at the time of the Mercy Flight;

Former CPA employee George Wells (St. Albert) who related many stories;

Engineer Ken Molson (Toronto) for colours and details of Aircraft;

Canada's Aviation Hall of Fame (Wetaskiwin), The Provincial Museum of Alberta (& staff Maurice Doll and Ted Smith), The Glenbow Museum (Calgary), The Prince of Wales Museum (Yellowknife), Alberta Archives (Edmonton), Carberry Plains Museum, Western Canada Aviation Museum (Winnipeg);

"Gumboots" of Yellowknife, N.W.T. for their permission to use their song about Wop May from their CD "Northern Tracks", Bob MacQuarrie who wrote the lyrics and Bill Gilday who wrote the music;

Owen Brierley of Edmonton for his work in developing the Wop May website which may be visited at; http://www.WopMay.com;

The Fort McMurray Historical Park where visitors can visit the house where Wop and Vi May lived;

Edward Zealley of Toronto, author, for his input into the chapter on The Mad Trapper;

The Canadian Aviation Historical Society; and

Sheila Reid, for her optimism, patience, perseverance and the many questions she asked.


Denny R. May
Edmonton, Alberta

# Prologue

The pain seared his chest and exploded, leaving behind a great crushing weight. He was not surprised, he just hadn't known when. He stopped, unfolded the seat of his walking cane, and called his son to him.

"You catch up with the others and make it to the cave. I'm going to stay here and catch the view for a bit."

He lowered himself onto his "shooting stick" and smiled at his son, waving him on. Then an idea came to him and he called: "Here, take my picture to show them I got this far."

Alone, he looked around and above him. A good day for a flight. He sat up straight with the anticipation he always had just before take-off, all senses alert, the machine throbbing under him, the sky beckoning above. He revved the engine, released the throttle, and was up...

# 1
## *The*
## Two Wilfrids

Birthplace of W.R. Wop May in Carberry, Manitoba. March 20, 1896.

It was 1896. The century was getting ready to close. There was a restlessness in the world. And there was hope, a universal expectation of something about to happen. Impossibilities about to be made possible. Time seemed on the verge of giving birth to a brand new life.

Canada was 29 years old. It had grown and filled out from coast to coast and had a railway to prove it. It held the promise of the New World. Gold was discovered at the rainbow's end in the Klondike, bringing a wave of immigrants into the new land with dreams of unlimited wealth for all. Easterners moved west as the promise of free farms lured families from the crowded unemployment of cities into the great fertile belt of the Canadian prairies. Prosperity was within everyone's grasp, was everyone's right. And the colony was talking nationhood.

In Ottawa, the air was crackling with debates on free trade and the French language bill. A cabinet was about to revolt and a government was about to fall.

Although the Province of Manitoba was hundreds of miles away from the Canadian capital, politics was a deeply moving force there as the population grew in strength and voice. People had come west with a dream of a new and better life and they were prepared to work for it no matter how far away they were from the political capital. They were already proving that they had the drive and determination to create Western Canada.

Many of those who boarded the settlement trains heading out of Southern Ontario liked the looks of the gently rolling Carberry Hills, and got off. By 1882 they felt settled enough to guarantee themselves a place on the CPR line by moving the nearest station to Carberry one dark night. This not only guaranteed them a stop for more settlers but a depot for incoming and outgoing trade. By 1889, Manitoba had gone from being an importer of flour to an exporter of wheat, proud of its one million acres of ploughed land and thirteen hundred miles of railway lines. By 1890, Carberry had become large enough to separate from the municipality of North Cypress and be incorporated as a village. It already had its own newspaper, the 1890 Christmas edition of which proudly reported

A.E. May & Company Carriages and Implements, Carberry, Manitoba, 1898.

that the town had twenty-six business houses plus a volume of merchant and blacksmith business amounting to $335,000.

It was a good time and place for an enterprising young man with a sense of

May's Service Station, E.C. May & Company Edmonton, Alberta (Jasper Ave., between 105 & 106th St.) early 1900's.

adventure and vision to be alive. A man like Alexander May who, by age twenty-five, had developed a well-established reputation for selling implements to town and country customers alike. Young May's success had been followed with interest by a large dealer in town, William Hunt, who had soon asked Alex to join him as an agent. When Hunt was elected to the first Carberry Town Council in April of 1890, he had been grateful to have Alex May looking after the business.

For his part, Alex realized that with his financial security finally in place, he could now venture into another arena. Twenty-five years was long enough for living alone, especially when he had already met the woman with whom he wanted to spend the rest of his life. She was Elizabeth Reid of Teeswater, Ontario, whose family had come to Canada from Scotland around the same time as the Mays had arrived from Ireland. Alex and Elizabeth had met just before the Mays made their move to the prairies and had carried on a long distance courtship ever since. Now, for the first time, he had a future to offer her. And so it was with a happy heart that he boarded the train for Southern Ontario to propose to her.

Alex and Elizabeth were married on June 10, 1891, at the home of Alex's business partner, William Hunt. Then they were off on a two-week honeymoon to Winnipeg and Brandon as Alex introduced his bride to the west.

Strengthened by his new union, Alex continued to prosper as he served the large and growing farming community. At home, the young couple became a family of four over the next two years as their son Elgin Court was born on June 15, 1892, and their daughter Vera Belle on October 22 the following year.

By the time 1896 began its march into history, the Conservative government of the country appeared to be losing its strength. As the smell of an election spread, the Liberals started gathering their forces. Alex May admired the political stand of Wilfrid Laurier, the Liberal leader in Ottawa. He saw Laurier as a man of vision and courage, the best man to end the twenty-two year Conservative reign in Parliament. His admiration of Laurier inspired him to get involved in politics himself. He and his wife would soon further honour the man who would become Canada's next prime minister by naming their third child after him.

With history hurrying towards the twentieth century, with Canada gathering its political forces for a summer election, with spring bursting forth from the grip of winter, Wilfrid Reid May made his entry into the world. It was March 20th, 1896.

# 2

# *The* Young Eagle
# Becomes Wop

Wilfrid Reid May, Edmonton, Alberta 1905.

In the protection and admiration of his family, Wilfrid May grew from baby to child. In the warming prairie sunshine he ripened into boyhood, testing his youthful vigour against the windswept landscape. Under the vast blue canopy of the prairie sky, he learned the freedom of space and wondered at the flight of an eagle that set his restless soul to stirring.

The high point in his day was the arrival of the daily train, announced by a far-off whistle that gave him the chance to race it to the station. It puffed and hissed at him as he dodged the flurry of activity that accompanied its stopping. He wondered where it had come from and where it was going.

His curiosity often took him beyond the edge of town, sometimes keeping him out

there until well after dark. He would frequently return with some new creature from the woods, in his arms if it was injured, always wanting to keep it, wanting his father to build a carriage for it. Each day brought a new adventure to the self-sufficient young explorer.

One day, he made a miracle happen. His mother lifted him up and told him to flick a switch on the wall. He did, and suddenly the lights came on at 43 Simcoe Street. He flicked the switch the other way and the lights went off. As if that wasn't enough to capture the full attention of an irrepressible five-year-old, one day he talked into a wooden box on the wall and heard his father's voice come all the way from Main Street, two blocks away.

With his father's growing involvement in politics, the atmosphere in the comfortable brick residence was constantly buzzing with the latest political issues. Mealtimes were almost always occasions for vigorous debates among the family and their many visitors, providing the opportunity for a small boy to serve himself double helpings of dessert. At night, as his eyes scanned the starry sky beyond his window, the voices of his parents and their friends drifted up to his bedroom, filling his ears and his imagination with dreams and possibilities for the future.

When Alex May was elected to the town council in 1899 and won the mayor's seat in 1901, his youngest child saw how dreams were set into motion. His father was the man who could make anything happen, his mother the security that kept things together as life sped ahead.

## The Family Heads West

Although politics continued to excite Alex May, success beyond the local municipal level eluded him at the polls. With his restless spirit stirring and no Liberal trip to Ottawa possible at the hands of the prairie voters, he turned his sights westward. His brother Charles had moved to Edmonton in the Northwest Territories a few years earlier, following his dream to set up a construction business. Charles had assured Alex of the endless opportunities in that thriving city with its many industries and its position as the purchasing centre of a large farming population. Ideal for a man who knew the farm implement business.

So it was that in the summer of 1903 the May family took its leave of Carberry and headed west.

The May family: Elizabeth & Alex, Vera, Court, Wilfrid. Edmonton, 1905.

It was on the way to their new home that Wilfrid became Wop. The family took a break in the long trip to visit relatives. A small two-year-old cousin found her way through the difficulties of saying "Wilfrid" by switching it to Wop, which she could say clearly. The reaction from everyone, including her seven-year-old cousin himself, was such that she used it again and again. By the end of the visit, Wilfrid had become Wop for the rest of his life.

As Wop grew through his youth and became a teenager in Edmonton, North America was growing too. In 1906, the continent discovered it had a Northwest Passage. In 1907, it discovered the space above its horizon line as Alexander Graham Bell's kite sailed into the skies above Baddeck, Nova Scotia, with a man attached to it. A year later, a man by the name of Frederick Walker (Casey) Baldwin became the first Canadian to fly an airplane. Two years later, the continent was ready for its first flying exhibition.

Vera, Alex & Wop May, Gull Lake, Alberta 1908.

Mobility was establishing itself on the ground as well, as cars were being built at the rate of two hundred a year and service stations opened up to fuel them. The world was on the move. The twentieth century was indeed under way, taking the world in a direction previously charted only by dreamers.

Who could sit still at a time like this? Wop barely managed to make it to the end of a school day as his mind raced ahead to the start of the day's real adventures. He would be the first one out of class at four o'clock, racing the short distance to his father's service station where there were cars to take apart and study. There had to be a way to make them go faster. His energetic determination eventually paid off as his speedometer registered the unheard-of speed of sixty miles an hour. When he wasn't waiting for the school day to end, he was counting the days to summer holidays. By this time the family had established a summer camp at Gull Lake, a

hundred miles south of the city, where the youngest member could put his high levels of restless energy into sailboats. He designed them, built them and raced them, challenging all comers.

And then one day in April a miracle flew into Edmonton that was to fuel the imagination of the fifteen-year-old forever. The Curtiss Pusher made its inaugural Alberta flight, taking off right above his head, then flying not once but five times around the area where he stood making him dizzy with exhilaration. To fly that fast, that high...well, the whole world would be yours, he thought.

With school never having held much excitement for the boy, the young man fought hard against his parents' push for him to do what they had never had a chance to do. Nonetheless, like it or not, he found himself on the train for Calgary right after high school, heading for Western Canada College and more school. It was only with the discovery of such extra-curricular pleasures as lacrosse and track that he settled into campus life. For a year. At that point, passing through the college library one day, his eye caught a picture in the newspaper. It showed a plane in action somewhere on the front lines of a war being fought somewhere far away. Nothing had ever captured his imagination and his need for challenge as much as that. Nothing ever would. He knew he would never be content until he was in that plane in that place. With that picture, he had seen what he wanted to do with his life. Nothing would get in his way. In no time at all he was off to join the war where men could fly.

Curtiss Pusher aircraft with Pilot Hugh Robinson, Edmonton Exhibition 1910. Wop May was likely in this crowd.

# 3

# Airborne *with* the Red Baron

The May Family, Edmonton 1917, before Wop went overseas.
Court, Vera, Alex, Elizabeth, Wilfrid.

As determined as he was to fly, Wop found it was not possible to get into a flying corps. Canada simply didn't have one. Undaunted, he decided to try another route. He enlisted in the infantry with the intention of transferring to the Royal Flying Corps when he got to England. It was his first lesson in military discipline as he quickly discovered that no one told the army what to do. And so he learned to march, to salute, to shoot, and to obey orders. Always he waited for his chance to get out and get up in the air.

Relentless in making his ambition known, Wop finally got accepted into the Royal Flying Corps School of Instruction at Acton near the end of the year. But he wasn't off the ground yet, as he soon found out. He first had to learn how to move the Caudron G3 trainer on the ground, how to start it and stop it, and how to balance its fragile bamboo wings. So he taxied down the field and back again as often as he could. At night he listened to the flyers tell of their adventures and fell asleep dreaming his dream of being one of them.

Finally, on November 17, 1917, his instructor got out of the Caudron and gave Wop his orders to take the plane up and show what he could do with it.

Released from the ground at long last, Wop wasted no time in getting up and testing his first piece of sky. Totally suspended, it made him heady to be part of this new space above the ground. At last he was the eagle racing the wind. He stretched his wings and soared, wanting to touch it all now that the dream was in motion. He also had an instructor to please, however, so he executed all the scheduled patterns with precision, growing more and more sure of himself.

It didn't take Wop's instructor long to recognize his student's flying ability and he soon gave the signal to bring the plane in for a landing. Wop acknowledged the order and made a smooth adjustment of the throttle to carry it out. But suddenly it seemed too fine a day to end such a perfect flight. Surely there would be bonus points for some extra manoeuvres, some pilot creativity. So he made another smooth adjustment of the throttle, sending the fragile craft into the heavens once more to complete a figure eight, then another, and yet another. He completed the performance with a perfect landing in a field nearby, right side up.

He cut his engine and leaped out of the plane, exhilarated from the triumph of his first solo flight, eager to receive the praise of his instructor. But to his great surprise, he was met by a whole chain of commanding officers who were looking for skill and obedience in the pilots they were preparing for battle. Not creativity. Wop was confined to quarters except for marching duty.

Time, persistence, and the obvious natural flying ability of the young man from Canada eventually got him through his training and at last he was given permission to take another solo. This time, the Avro 504K would be his machine. He knew he could count on its rotary engine to get him up to 20,000 feet and he was no stranger to its speed and manoeuvrability.

Wop gave the plane a reassuring pat and climbed into its small wicker seat. He taxied the Avro to the take-off point, revved the engine, and headed up into the sky. There was, after all, a war to be fought.

## Out and In Again

On March 23, 1918, he graduated from the 94 Squadron with a grand total of five and a half hours of flying time under his wings. But by April 9, with another 39 hours logged, plus training in formation flying and a gunnery course, he had earned himself a posting to the 209 Squadron.

The event marked the end of a long, tense grind for the twenty-two-year-old who had struggled hard to achieve his dream. And it was still wartime. Life held no guarantees beyond the moment at hand. All in all, it was an event that rated a celebration. With the help of his new-found buddies, it became the graduation party of the season as they turned night into day, and turned off the war. The two-day event became a three-day event, but not with the military's blessing. When Wop reported in for duty he found himself facing a very stern British Commanding Officer and an unceremonious dismissal from the squadron. It was not a good start for his eagerly awaited flying career and it was certainly not something a young man could write home about. Feeling like an errant schoolboy as he left the CO's office, Wop wondered how to get himself out of this quandary, how to get himself back up into the sky.

As he rounded the corner, completely preoccupied with his problem, he bumped into someone wearing a Captain's rank. He looked up, ready with an immediate apology, even a

Lieutenant W.R. May, Graduate pilot. Royal Flying Corps School of Instruction, March 1918. Acton, England. Aircraft is a Caudron G. III (G.3)

It had taken five months for Wop to go from a rookie enlisted infantryman to a fully trained fighter pilot. Five long months for a young man worried that the war would end before he could get into it. He would have five months in active combat before the war was officially over.

For the first month he kept a log of his flights. Then, like most flyers, he quit keeping records. With the odds against them returning to home base, it seemed pointless. His first combat flight rated only a short sparse note in his log book:

*April 20, 1918. First time on line. Flight got into scrap with triplane. Archied slightly. I didn't get a burst into them.*

Despite being shot at ("archied"), the young fighter pilot was up in the air again the next day. It would be the longest day of his life. Almost the last.

Manfred von Richthofen, the Red Baron, was well known to Wop. The German pilot's reputation of eighty kills made him a flying ace on both sides of the war. His exploits were discussed over many a late night drink in the airmens' quarters. Although his flying ability was admired by the flyers who encountered him in the air, his tactics were not. His strategy was to hold a position high above the fighting so he could not be seen. From that vantage point, he could watch the fighting of the fifty machines in his circuit as well as watch for crippled aircraft wearing the enemy's colours. When he spotted a plane that had been hit, he would move into action to finish off the kill. These tactics earned him no admiration from the Allied pilots, who

salute if necessary, and found himself looking into the face of an old school buddy from Edmonton, Roy Brown. It was a welcome reunion for both of them in this war zone so far away from home. For Wop, it became the means by which he won a second chance to get into the air fight of the First World War. The CO agreed to reinstate the young flyer under the charge of Captain Brown, who was also to be his Squadron Leader. It was to become the first of many successful ventures shared by these two Canadian flying aces.

Captain W.R. Wop May home after the war. Edmonton, Alberta 1919.

upheld a strict code of honour: you don't shoot a cripple and you keep it a fair fight.

As Wop woke up to his second day of active combat duty, there was talk of another airborne Richthofen. The Baron's young nephew had just acquired his flying papers. Wop felt an empathy with this fellow rookie even though they were fighting on opposite sides. The high excitement of finally getting the chance to be in the air was mixed with the frustration of being on probation, under strict orders to remain above the action to watch and learn. Wop was impatient with being a rookie for the second day in a row. But he was aware that he had run out of second chances. Roy Brown, friend on the ground, was Captain Roy Brown, Squadron Leader in the air. His command to "sit up high and watch" would be reluctantly obeyed by his newest rookie.

## Into the Enemy Zone

Being in the machine with its engine roaring in his ears gave Wop back the feeling of power. At least he would be in the air somewhere near the fighting. He taxied with the others and rose into the air as one of them.

Spotting no enemy aircraft, the squadron entered the German air zone. Fifteen...twenty miles...and then there they were, down below. Forty or fifty of the colourfully painted planes. The enemy. Brown waggled the wing of his aircraft, the signal into action, and the Royal Air Force swooped into battle. Wop's hands moved instinctively to follow when Roy's words echoed in his ear. He headed for the sun.

It was difficult to distinguish one plane from the next at such a distance above the action. And difficult to watch what was happening with the smoke and the roaring and crashing of the battle. Suddenly, just below

Lieutenent W.R. May in Sopwith Camel, France, 1919.

him, Wop spotted a German plane flying, like him, alone and above the battle. A fellow rookie? The nephew? He headed toward him, glad of the company. But the German pilot swung away with no return greeting.

It was becoming intolerably lonely for the anxious flyer as he listened to the sounds of battle, impatient to be there with his buddies. Boot camp or no, there's only so much waiting in an eager young man. When the German plane made another appearance, Wop let go a warning shot at it, then decided to follow it and try another shot. As he came out of the cloud cover, he suddenly found himself in the centre of the German circuit. They wasted no time in showing him he was in enemy territory. He watched them closing in on him from all sides, and decided the best way out of the mess was to go into a tight vertical turn, hold his guns open and spray as many as he could. He began

to do that but in his nervousness and inexperience he held his guns open too long. One jammed, then the other. With no time left to make them work, Wop spun around and headed west into the sun, fully expecting a blast in the back of his neck at any second. When he finally stopped his dizzy spinning and levelled off, he was surprised to find that he was still alive, and alone.

He breathed a sigh of relief, grateful to have escaped such an attack, and was wondering what his next move should be when a bullet landed on his wing from the rear. Then another. He turned around in his seat to see where his attacker was. It was a red triplane and it was close. Clearly, it was time to move in a new direction, down, and attempt to dodge the German's fire.

So, down Wop dodged and dived, twelve thousand feet or more, until he ran out of sky

The entry for April 21, 1918, from Wop's logbook describing his air battle with the Red Baron.

## THE GIANTS

This Episode: Wilfred "Wop" May

From a comic strip by Walt McDayter and Norman Drew, Calgary *Herald*, October 1965.

and was scratching his plane's belly on the hedges along the road. The firing continued from his flying assailant as well as from the ground troops. With his own guns not working and his attacker heavy on his tail, the best he could do would be to stay beyond reach, and hope. For fifteen miles he hedge-hopped, slipping and sliding, one eye on the hedge ahead and one on the roaring machine behind him. The skin on the back of his neck was rubbed raw by this time as he tried to keep his pursuer in sight.

When he saw that they had passed over to Allied lines, he breathed a sigh of relief. He had made it with only a couple of holes in his wings to show for the attack...

Crack!

Wop swung around. He was still being chased, and in the brief second of his thinking it was over, his attacker had gained the sky above him. Turning back to see where he was heading and where he could quickly dodge, he saw that he was very close to taking a plunge into the Somme River. The hilly banks allowed him no room to turn away. He headed up the valley at a very low altitude and rounded the curve of the river, only to see

that the red triplane had taken a shortcut over the hill and was coming right down into him.

The reality of his situation made him freeze with fear. He had run out of chances, out of dodges, out of luck, seemingly out of life. The best he could do now was to make sure his pursuer didn't take the credit for the kill. He would take himself down. He put his hand on the stick to plunge himself and his machine into the river, took one last look around him, and saw the German plane hit the ground, crashing on impact. Above it, was a plane wearing his own colours. Lifting his machine up into the air, he recognized his rescuer, none other than his Squadron Leader. They exchanged greetings, then the high sign to fly up and away to home base.

Wop could barely wait to bring his machine to a full stop in order to leap out and catch up with Roy. More than anything, he needed Roy to know that he hadn't meant to start what Roy had finished. The Squadron Leader listened to his rookie flyer defend the incredible flight that he himself had witnessed. Then he commended Wop on the way he had kept his aircraft well out of reach for so long, long enough to keep the German pilot from

Baron Manfred von Richtofen, The Red Baron.

Australian riflemen firing volley over Richtofen's grave.

realizing he himself was being pursued. As good a flyer as the German was, he had neglected to check his bearings and his attack zones, and had thus made himself vulnerable to attack.

Wop was suddenly very aware that he was alive at that moment because of Roy Brown. For the first time, he understood how much he still had to learn about this flying business, and how much he owed the man beside him. This new knowledge would help make him the flying ace that Roy Brown believed him to be.

It was some time later that both pilots learned the identity of the one who had given them such a chase. None other than Baron von Richthofen, known internationally as the Red Baron. When Wop finally made his way into bed that night, he took his log book and recorded the events of the day's battle:

> *April 21. Engaged 15 - 20 triplanes.*
> *Claimed one. Blue one. Several*
> *on my tail. Came out with red triplane on*
> *my tail. Guns were jammed.*

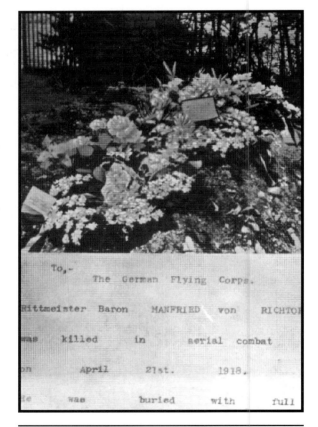

Notification sent to the German Flying Corps announcing the death of Richtofen.

Translation  of Telegram send by Generalobert v. Georing

J convey to you the sincerest united thanks of the German
Aviators and the entire German Nation, for the fragment of Baron von
Richthovens Airoplane which today was handed over to us by a Com -
mission of the Canadian Olympic Committee.   I reciprocate in the
name of my Aviation Comrades and all of my countrymen the friendly
feelings which this presentation conveyed to us and greet you most
sincerely in Comradeship
                                Goering      Generaloberst.


Text of Telegram send to Generaloberst v. Goering.

To you, the German Aviation and people sincerest thanks for your
friendly and honorable feelings and trust that the Olympic games
now on progress will further cement the  happy relations now existing
between Grmany and Canada.
                          Captain W.R. May

Translation into German :

Jhnen dem deutschen Luftwesen und Volke aufrichtigsten Dank
fuer Ihre kameradschaftlichen und edelen Gefuehlen. Jn Anbetracht
der Olympischen Spiele soll Dieses noch mithelfen das freundschaftliche
Verstaendnis zwischen Deutschland und Canada mehr zu festigen.
                          Captain W.R. May

Telegram from General Goering thanking Wop May for returning fragment of Baron von Richtofen's aircraft & reply. The Edmonton "Grads" Basketball Team took the fragment to the Berlin Olympics in 1936.

*Tripe on my tail all the time. Got several bursts into me but didn't hit me. When we got across the line he was shot down by Capt. Brown.*

*I saw him crash into side of hill. Came back with Capt. We afterward found out that the triplane (red) was famous German airman Baron Richthofen. He was killed.*

He closed the book and fell asleep. It had been a full day.

## Who Shot The Red Baron?

In terms of history, it was the beginning of a new legend. The air chase between the Red Baron and the two Canadians was the stuff of stories told and retold in troop bunks and officers' quarters, spread over airwaves throughout the world, gaining a place in history books forever. It was to become a major event of the war, one for which everyone wanted to claim the credit. According to Wop's account, it was Captain Brown's plane that he gratefully witnessed bringing down the Red Baron. Brown's report stated that he fired one short burst from behind and above the Baron. But there was also a group of Australians who claimed the credit for the final flight of the renowned German ace. They had been positioned on the ground where the Baron and Wop were hedge-hopping. An Australian gunner on top of the hill who was firing at the red German triplane claimed that it was his marksmanship that finally brought it down. The autopsy report showed that the bullet entered from behind and came out the chest, passing through or near his heart, killing him instantly.

Wop's squadron dropped the message at a German airport that their flying legend had been killed and that he had been buried in a lead coffin at Bertangles Cemetery with full military honours. They also dropped flowers, a traditional flyer's farewell. Wop brought home the strut from Richthofen's Fokker as part of his wartime memorabilia. In 1936, he cut the strut in two and sent half to Richthofen's mother on the occasion of the Olympic Games as an official gesture of goodwill between the two nations. For that he received an official telegram of appreciation from Herman Goering. Ironically, within three years, the two countries would be once more on opposing sides with the outbreak of yet another great war.

With luck and a combined skill at handling aircraft and aerial marksmanship, Wop managed to stay alive and put thirteen or more enemy aircraft out of commission before the war was over. He also found time to write home about it.

---

### May 18

Dear folks

We have had quite a bit of excitement lately. I am with the other flights until we get another flight fixed up again. I was up testing my machine yesterday and the engine blew up. Tore the cowling off and flung it on to my left hand flying wires. Something blew out and hit my right wing and ripped it. Side plate and covering were hanging all over the machine. The main trouble was the covering on the left wing caused so much wind resistance.

Had quite a job getting it under control, but managed o.k. and landed at the drome.

Wop

---

*May 22.*

Dear folks

Good flying weather. Just got new flight commander. This is the fourth since I came. I hope Capt. Brown will be here again soon. We were on the night flying stunt again this morning. I like flying at night. It's great to watch the sun rising at twelve to fourteen thousand feet up. It rises sooner there than down stairs. It has been very hot lately and it is a relief to get up in the cool air. You may not think it possible to get frozen under these conditions. I froze my face the other day. It is nearly better now.

It was at 21,000 feet I got it. My wind screen was bust - that's why. It's a lovely morning. Perfectly peaceful. You wouldn't think there was a war on at all.

Wop

---

*May 27.*

Dear folks

Well, I had a little luck today on this side of the line. I got a two-seater. I was up the line to see it this afternoon and to see if I could get any crosses, etc. but there was not much left of it. It came down in flames. I am sending you a piece of the wing covering material, a linen fabric, coloured in varied neutral tints.

Wop

---

*May 29.*

Dear folks

Not much doing today. Our flight didn't have anything. I took a flip up to see the Canadians this evening but did not land. It was too windy. Took three-quarters of an hour to go and fifteen minutes to come back, so you can imagine how windy it was. My speed coming back wasn't slow. Have a new machine now. This is my third. No. I didn't crash them. I just wore them out. It does not take long on this job. You throw them around so much and drive them so fast it soon puts them on the hum.

Wop

---

*May 31,*

Dear folks

They have kept us on the go lately but we are having lots of fun so we don't complain. We had a chase this morning. Some chase too. Got off the ground in two minutes. Got over about six miles. (Flying in threes, flight commander in charge of three). Sent two two-seaters east and then came back. On the way back took a drag at a balloon.

Fritz didn't like it and sure gave me a warm time. Was alone so all attention was on me. The Archie is pretty good at 6000. But they are very easily fooled, thank goodness, and it's great fun fooling them.

Wop

---

When the armistice was finally signed, the battle-weary troops put down their guns and listened to the silence. It was not Wop's way of celebrating. He raced to his plane, started up the engine, and headed into the skies one more time. But this time in an aerial dance, not in battle. He aimed for the steeple at the centre of the town and soared around it. As he noticed the gathering townsfolk and infantry troops down below him, he waved his white scarf and led them in a victory cheer. Then he showed them how a young pilot from Canada celebrated being alive at such a moment, with swoops and loops of aerial exuberance, free at last to enjoy a sky at peace. It was only when his gas gauge reached "empty" that he brought himself back to earth. And he finally agreed to let the hospital staff start the big job of digging the shrapnel out of his arms and chest, which he had acquired on his many combat missions and ignored.

Despite Wop's late entry into the war, his efforts managed to win him the Distinguished Flying Cross with the citation from King George VI:

> This officer has carried out numerous offensive and low-bombing patrols, proving himself on all occasions a bold and daring pilot... His keenness and disregard of personal danger is worthy of the highest praise.

He was also awarded the Victory Medal, for surviving the war, and the Great War Medal for being in it. To Canadians, he was celebrated as a Flying Ace with the shooting of thirteen enemy aircraft to his credit. On receiving the accolades and the hero's welcome on his return home, however, Wop's response was always:

> *It was war. We were defending our country. We had a strict code of honour: you didn't shoot a cripple and you kept it a fair fight.*

## THE GIANTS

This Episode: Wilfred "Wop" May

McDayter and Drew, Calgary *Herald*, October 1965.

# 4

# Barnstorming
# *and* Other Stunts

**Wop May's pilot licence No. 49. July 7, 1919.**

**Wop May's commercial pilot licence No. 7. May 7, 1920.**

Finally, the war was over and the world returned to normal.

The Mays welcomed back their son, grateful for his safe return. Even with the close scrutiny of parents, they could find no traces of the boy who had left in this man who now stood before them, his face wearing the squint lines of those who flew so close to the sun. They hoped he had had his fill of flying and fighting, that he would now settle down and help them expand the family business that sold and serviced MacLaughlin cars. It was soon clear, however, that World War flying aces wanted to find jobs in civilian skies. If they were good and took risks, they barnstormed. If they were lucky, they didn't get killed at it.

Wop was good, and he was lucky. Just before the end of the war, his brother Court had started a commercial flying business.

May Airplanes Limited, Curtiss JN4-D *Edmonton.* May Field , 1919.

## EDMONTON JOURNAL

# AIRPLANE EXHIBITION

Lieut. Geo. Gorman of Edmonton

has just completed the

**First Air Delivery of Journals to Wetaskiwin**

The Airplane is the Curtis Military Triplane "City of Edmonton," painted with the markings of the Royal Air Force as used on active service.

# Saturday, June 7th
1919

Copy of original brochure advertising the first air delivery of the *Edmonton Journal* from Edmonton to Wetaskiwin. June 7, 1919. Note the error identifying the aircraft as a "Triplane".

enough for them to call themselves May Airplanes. They continued to rent the city's Jenny, for its wings could handle the stress of quick turns, loops, and rolls which daredevil flying demanded. "Wop May" was painted on the top in large letters so it could be read when he flew the plane upside down.

Most barnstormers made an appearance wherever there was most likely to be a crowd of people. There, they did their stunts, which often included having someone hanging on to a wing. When they had attracted enough of a crowd, they landed and offered rides. The May brothers, however, did it their way. They would write to a town telling what they were prepared to do and the town either hired them or didn't. With their growing reputation for flying stunts, they were hired more often than not. Wop became a feature attraction at fairs and circuses in Edmonton and nearby towns, a dashing and daring hero dressed in his battle uniform, complete with cap, goggles, and flying white scarf. His most popular stunts were looping the loop, zooming, half rolling,

With the flying ace back home, they were ready to go public together. They rented a Curtiss Jenny from the City of Edmonton for $25 a month, posted a $1000 performance bond, and went into business to perform low-flying daredevil antics. By May, 1919, business was good

Wop May with Len Adair's Curtiss JN4-D Jenny. Name on top was so it could be seen when he was flying the aircraft upside down.

Wop May in flying gear with Len Adair's Jenny at Calgary.

Wop May with two admirers.

full rolling, upside-down flying, and the spinning nose-dive. Posters advertising the flying exhibition claimed there was nothing that could be done with any machine "that our pilots do not perform several times." There was an "absolute guarantee" that the audience would see everything worthwhile in airplane stunts.

A newspaper account of Wop's performance in Grande Prairie on August 26, 1920, was headlined:

CAPT. WOP MAY'S AEROPLANE WAS LEADING ATTRACTION AT GRANDE PRAIRIE EXHIBITION LAST WEEK".
Friday at 11:30 a.m. Captain Wop May appeared on the eastern horizon in the first aeroplane to make the trip from Edmonton to the Grande Prairie district, and was the centre of at-

traction during the fair and is continuing in the same role. After pulling off a few hair-raising stunts over the exhibition grounds, he commenced carrying passengers and has been the busiest man in the country ever since. The traffic was continued all day Saturday, the captain not being able to even get time for dinner until night had closed in. All day Sunday was spent in the same way, large crowds being lined up awaiting their turn. A large waiting list still remains and it looks like the captain is to have an indefinite stay if all the would-be fliers in the city have their ambitions gratified. It is unquestionably the most popular attraction that has appeared in the north country, and the directorate of the exhibition is being congratulated in bringing Captain May north. On arrival, he delivered mail from the premier, the president of the Edmonton Board of Trade, Acting Mayor East and other prominent citizens of Edmonton.

Wop May in Curtiss JN4-D Jenny. Edmonton, 1920.

Local people inspecting Wop May's Jenny at the Grande Prairie Fair, August 20, 1920.

## Never Stuck for Long

One such tour of flying exhibitions ended up in the muskeg. With his mechanic Pete Derbyshire, Wop was returning home from a successful six-week tour to Grande Prairie, Peace River, Waterhole, and Spirit River. Near Whitecourt their engine died and they were forced to land. Unsettled, unfamiliar, and unfriendly, the area contained no answer to their problem. Rather, as it turned out, more problems.

They had spotted the Athabasca River from the air and judged it close enough to reach. However, they didn't quite find the river and the dense muskeg in which they landed seemed intent on keeping them lost. After wandering around for a day and a half, they finally had to accept the inevitable: they were stuck until they fixed their machine.

The job tested the skills of both pilot and mechanic as they taped, patched, and wired, fashioning new pieces from old. And it worked. The engine started. Their victory, unfortunately, was short-lived. The wheels were deeply stuck by this time in the high muskeg. But they'd come too far to let that stop them now. Recognizing that they needed to lighten their load, they struck a deal. Pete would get out and push, and then walk out to the river with Wop flying overhead showing the way. It worked and they were on their way home at last, following the elusive Athabasca which as it turned out was only a short distance from where they had landed in the first place.

The May airplane became a familiar sight in the air over Edmonton when it wasn't off on tour. It frequently halted downtown traffic, baseball games, and Sunday drives, as Edmontonians stopped to marvel at how it got up and how it stayed up. When it was on the ground, they closed in for a better look. They touched its thin cloth cover. They examined the wire braces that held its wings and tail together. They climbed up and peeked into the open cockpit to see for themselves the control stick, the rudder pedals, the throttle, the gas gauge, the compass, the few instruments on the small instrument panel. As they climbed back down they shook their heads in amazement, their curiosity greater than ever.

But the plane never stayed on the ground for long, and where it went the press was sure to follow.

On July 12, 1919, Edmonton's Diamond Ball Park was ready for its official opening.

The *Edmonton* over the Tegler Building, Edmonton - 1919/20.

Wop flying Mayor Joe Clarke over Diamond Park to throw the first ball of the season. Edmonton, 1919. They flew under the High Level Bridge on the way to the field!

The ceremonial pitch was to be thrown by Mayor Joe Clarke from Wop May's moving plane. Giving this mission his usual amount of careful planning, Wop decided that the best angle for the mayor to throw the pitch was from the river side, and the only way to do that was to approach the park along the river from the west. The one obstacle to this plan that Wop could foresee was the location of the high-level bridge. But, he reasoned, if the bridge could be flown over, it could be flown under as well. And under the bridge they flew to give a somewhat surprised mayor the best angle to throw the ceremonial and history-making pitch.

## Take-off on Main Street

Always, Wop kept one eye on the future. When he wasn't performing his stunts, he was introducing aviation services to Western Canada. Aerial photography, for one. Started during the war to provide information about strategic enemy locations, aerial photography was seen to have many peacetime uses as well. The first aerial photo of the University of Alberta was taken by Wop May of May Airplanes Limited.

Aerial police work was another service that Wop got into one day when a detective knocked on his door. A criminal who was wanted for murdering an Edmonton policeman had been seen heading for the mining towns of the Alberta Coal Branch south of Edson. To reach the area as quickly as possible, hopefully before the criminal, the detective hired Wop to fly him to Edson.

The unfamiliar drone of an airplane motor in the sky brought everyone in Edson outside to see what was going on. By the time the plane landed, Wop had himself an admiring crowd. The detective, clearly not the subject of the admiration, climbed out of the passenger's seat unnoticed and headed over to the station to catch the train for the Coal Branch. The townspeople kept Wop busy answering their questions. What made his airplane fly? How would he get it off the ground again? And because it was his machine and he was proud to fly it, Wop answered all the questions, responding warmly to their excitement.

With the only open and level piece of ground being the two blocks on Main Street in front of the Edson Hotel, landing had been difficult. The take-off, however, would require a longer strip of level and open ground. Someone suggested using the main street. Wop looked it over and agreed. He was glad there was no wind and no overhead wires to tangle up his machine. Only a town pump in the middle of the street to contend with. He had a couple of men hold the wings at each end as he taxied up the street, but there wasn't enough room to clear the pump and one of the wings got nicked. A quick survey of the damage showed it wasn't serious, so they continued to the end of the street where the plane was turned around.

By this time the entire community was involved. Someone arrived with several five-gallon cans of gasoline to refuel the plane. A man came up from the railroad office to crank the motor. He had just returned from overseas and knew how to do it, he explained. But then the final part of this community event was up to Wop. He took off down the street at full tilt, cleared the town pump, and was off the ground with a hearty wave to the Edson folk who stood and watched until the plane was out of sight and they could hear it no more. It was a show they would never forget.

## May-Gorman Partnership

Unfortunately, for even such an energetic and enterprising pilot, expenses were higher than the money made and the May brothers were forced to seek the partnership of George Gorman to stay in business. Wop and George had shared some air fighting overseas before George had been brought down and taken prisoner by the Germans. Now he was ready for more, so the May-Gorman Aeroplanes Ltd. company was established. Their operations included an extensive delivery route for newspapers and mail to service the needs of farmers, miners, and loggers throughout central Alberta.

The comings and goings from the May Field were excitedly reported by the press which had a reading audience hungry for news about these explorers of the skies. When the Imperial Oil Company needed some planes brought north to service their new oil discovery sites near the Arctic, they knew who to call

George Gorman accepting the *Edmonton Journal* for delivery by air to Wetaskiwin, 1919. May-Gorman Aeroplanes Ltd.

# ~ Giant ~ Monoplane and Party!

### 5 Men Land in Edmonton

### 5.20 p.m.

### Wednesday

### Completing Winter Trip from New York

upon for the job. Although it was close to Christmas, both Wop and George were ready for a new adventure and accepted the invitation to travel to New York to pick up the two planes. The fact that it was winter, the fact that it was a long way from New York to Edmonton, the fact that such a flight had never been attempted before, all added to the adventure for both pilots. Off they set for New York by train to meet these new models.

Wop had never seen such a plane. It was a low wing Junkers monoplane with an all-metal body, a wing spread of forty-eight feet, and a weight of a little more than a ton. There was room for six passengers in an enclosed cabin which, to Wop, looked more like a car than any plane he had ever seen before. He climbed into the pilot's seat and revved the motor, enjoying the sound of its 170-horsepower heart. He could hardly wait to see if it really could pull off the ground carrying its own weight.

Wop May with Imperial Oil's Junkers-Larsen JL-6 following the flight from New York.

Once the news came that Wop and George were heading home, Edmonton eagerly read the progress reports in the press as they made it safely through Belfontaine, Sandusky, Cleveland, Chicago, Minneapolis, and Brandon. When the planes landed at Saskatoon, the press reported a delay due to heavy icing of the wings and propellers as well as the need to heat the oil for the engines in the cold winter temperatures. At last, word came that they were leaving Saskatoon. The crowd gathered to welcome them home, lighting a large bonfire at the aerodrome to offset the cold January wind. In the meantime, the flyers had put down midway for fuel. As they took off for the home stretch, Gorman's machine got caught on a fence, causing damage to its undercarriage and forcing Gorman to settle in for the repairs that were needed.

On his own for the first time during this long flight, and facing a strong west wind which drove harder and harder against the thrust of his machine, Wop knew he was losing time and daylight. With the growing darkness, he realized that he would have to execute a straight landing despite his inclination to end this historic transcontinental flight with a fancy finale.

Cheers went up with the flames from the welcoming party as Edmonton's flying hero taxied the giant plane toward them. Wop bedded the plane down and went to meet the press, tired, cold, and stiff, but enthusiastic about the machine he had handled for the last five hours. He had high praise for its performance in difficult conditions. As he told the press, "I can heartily endorse its use in the rough conditions of the north. I can and I will

Local people with Imperial Oil's Junkers-Larsen JL-6. Back Row (L-R) - Charles Taylor (in charge of production, Imperial Oil), Tronson & Mrs Draper, Alex McQueen (VP in charge of construction for Imperial Oil), Dick Myers. Front Row (L-R) Pilots George Gorman and Wop May.

safely predict that you, members of the press, are looking at the machine that will open up the north. But I can also assure you that I will not be the one to take it there. I'm heading home to sleep. Possibly forever. Good evening, gentlemen."

The *Bulletin* of January 6, 1921, proudly proclaimed the flight "a historical turning point made by the Edmonton boys, for they have opened up a scheme of transportation that requires neither paved roads nor steel rails."

As Wop had predicted, he was not the one to fly the plane into the north. It was left up to Gorman and another pilot to complete the delivery of the Junkers. Wop had to wait until Gorman's return in the spring to hear the full account of that part of the trip. He listened eagerly as Gorman described the natives' reaction to their first sight of an airplane heading in for a landing. Some had looked at it as their "Thunderbird."

Wop was particularly interested in Gorman's account of the repair to a splintered propeller. Pressing Gorman for the details, he learned that they had fashioned a propeller out of a sleigh board and made a glue out of moose hides to hold it together. Wop was excited to hear that such a makeshift prop could not only stand a strain of 1500 revolutions a minute from a 175-horsepower engine, but also be able to drive a heavy machine through the air at 90 miles an hour. Although the whole ordeal had convinced his partner that the north was no place for their planes, it proved to Wop that the north was the direction they should go. There were business ventures and payloads to take them there in their flying machines.

Despite Gorman's protests, Wop put together a prospectus to sell their services to northern investors:

> The Great North Service Company has taken over the assets, business and goodwill of the May-Gorman Aeroplanes Ltd. to establish an aerial transportation service between Fort McMurray and Fort Norman. Boasting authorized capital of $100,000; a Board of Directors featuring DSO's, geologist, mine owner, and Eastern Canadian brokers and advisors.
> First consideration to be given to the safety and comfort of passengers and reliability of service. Flying Boats to cruise at 75 mph. Liberty motors of 400 hp. To ensure safety will follow water route and cover 1000 miles in 34 hours allowing for stops and windage. Intention to equip Flying Boats with wireless. Capt. Wop May, whose experience and ability in the air service is well known, will be in charge of the

Company's Flying Boats. Assets of May-Gorman Aeroplanes Ltd. at this time: 1 new Curtiss aeroplane, 1 parachute, 1 complete set of spare parts and 1 hangar to be exchanged for 150 fully paid-up shares of Great North Services Ltd. @$100 each share.

But it would remain a dream for another few years.

In completing his part of the Junkers flight from New York to Edmonton, Wop had proved to aviation that cross-country flight was possible in any season. He had accomplished this six years before Charles Lindberg was to cross the Atlantic and make his historical contribution to aviation. Wop had also proved something about himself. At twenty-five, he was now to be taken seriously as a pilot with exceptional skills. He knew that he could feel part of any plane he climbed into and as quickly become master of its controls. Although the press would continue to love his daring, they would now begin to recognize his maturity of purpose. By so doing, they would start to take aviation seriously. They would continue to track the flights of Wop May, but these would no longer be called "stunts." They would be recognized for what they were to become. Missions.

# 5

# Hurdles *of a* Personal Kind

Wop and Vi May - married November 19, 1924, Edmonton, Alberta

Something else was beginning to happen in Wop's life that would temporarily replace flying as the centre of his world.

It all started at a horse show, unfamiliar turf to a pilot. A friend had asked him to come along to it, and, with no flying engagements on his calendar, he agreed. Many admiring eyes followed the famous flyer into the show ring while he, always intent on learning something new, concentrated on the form and motion of the horses and their riders. One rider in particular began to attract his attention as she entered the ring and guided her mount over the series of obstacles. They cleared the hurdles as one, in a rhythmic flow of motion, reminding him of the synchronism of a pilot and his plane.

As she completed her rounds and came out of the ring, Wop walked over to her. She was flushed with the success of the ride and her eyes danced with exhilaration. A few wisps of beautiful dark hair showed from under her fashionable rider's cap. Wop was momentarily caught off guard by her beauty and was at a loss for words. Recovering, he shyly introduced himself and was rewarded by the sound of her deep rich voice with its soft British accent as she told him her name. Violet Bode. He congratulated her on her ride. She acknowledged with a smile that reached deep within him. In a spontaneous burst of inspiration, he reached into his pocket, pulled out his good luck charm and gave it to her for her next round. She accepted the gesture and put the charm in the pocket of her riding vest. Then it was time for her final ride.

Wop stood in intense anticipation with the other spectators and watched as rider and horse proceeded to jump over, and knock down, all the hurdles, one by one. None were cleared. When the ill-fated ride was finally finished, Violet walked her horse over to the abashed young man and silently handed him back his good luck charm.

At best, Wop hoped he could get back up into the air and disappear as soon as possible. At next best, he hoped he would never run into her again. But destiny had very different plans for this flyer. A few months later he walked into the City Commissioner's office and found himself facing a new receptionist. This time there was no need for introductions. It was none other than Miss Violet Bode.

Violet's passion for horses and equestrian accomplishments had started in England where she, like many English children, had her own pony. When her banker father died of tuberculosis in 1913, her mother had moved with her two daughters to Canada, first to Victoria, then to Calgary, finally to Edmonton. Violet was never long in finding a stable wherever they went. However, her equestrian activities were expensive. To finance her horse show circuits and her polo training, she worked wherever she could.

Between flights, Wop had always spent a lot of time in his family's shop, indulging his curiosity about engines and helping with jobs that could always use an extra hand. Now he began to visit the City Commissioner more often, for the young woman in the office had

captured his imagination. He liked her quick and quiet wit, her love of adventure, and the charm and grace of her beauty. When she smiled and said his name, he was captivated. As he learned more about her reputation as an equestrienne and her successes on various polo teams, he respected the passion and the determination, the spirit and the courage, of this unique lady.

Whether it was the shirt and tie he always wore in and out of an airplane, or the intensity of his blue eyes as he searched to learn more than he knew already, Wop's initial bad luck with the lady changed over the next three years to become a close friendship. She found time after feeding and watering her horses at the stable to drive down to May Field and provide him with landing lights from her borrowed car.

One night she was delayed at the stables. It was dark by the time she finally arrived at the airfield but the lights of her car found the man and his machine immediately, completely ensnared by a barbed wire fence. They both climbed out of their respective machines and met in the headlights of her car. As Wop put his arms around her, he realized just how much he needed this beautiful young woman in his life. He lost no time in telling her. Since her own heart had been set in motion for quite some time, she wondered what had taken him so long in discovering his own. But at this time and in this place, she merely looked up at him, smiled, and said yes.

## A November Wedding

If Wop had the romantic notion of a young flying adventurer to loop his beautiful sweetheart through the arch of a gold

November sunset and claim her as his wife, he soon found himself back on the ground. A wedding was a serious business in the Edmonton society of 1924. Not to mention a major social event when the principle participants have been so closely tracked by the media.

WARRIOR OF MANY BATTLES BOWS TO CUPID'S DICTATES proclaimed one headline. WOP CRASHES announced another. The press even became poetic about the whole event:

Tis claimed that in the days of war
The gentle Hun said he would pay
A dozen shining medals for
The person of one Wilfrid May.
"Alive or dead" the message ran
And all the guns turned out by Krupp
Were trained on Wop. That wild young man
Just kept on flying up and up.
They chased this reckless lad about
But more than one Hun airman found
He hadn't time to flatten out
Before he met the solid ground
For Wop knew how to squirt the lead –
As nice a shot as one could ask
Those men have been a long time dead;
To land May was a hopeless task.
But now he's crashed - no whizzing shell
Has brought him down or cramped his style
His epitaph will read: "He fell
Before a charming woman's smile."
And yet us single chaps won't sigh
Because he's left our ranks that way

We're all too glad to cheer and cry
"Good luck to Wop and Mrs. May!"

In the tradition of the time, the parlour of her mother's home was cleared and bedecked for the ceremony, and the dining room was set for the buffet reception, despite the fact that the bride-to-be would eat none of it due to an untimely onslaught of lockjaw from tetanus!

At precisely 8 o'clock on November 24, Wop caught the first sight of his bride and once again was awestruck with her beauty and her regal bearing as she made her way toward him. He smiled when he saw the rope of pearls he had given her shining like moondrops around her neck. She looked up into his sky blue eyes and knew she was about to take off on the flight of a lifetime.

With a bride to provide for, and with his family encouraging him to settle down in a safe place on the ground, Wop went about looking for a steady job. He knew that it would be a few years before a career in flying would be anything more than sporadic, and there were other things that he knew how to do. Growing up with his family's business so close at hand, he had gained a wide reputation as a mechanic who could fix anything that moved in the air or on the ground.

## A Shot in the Eye

A job offer soon came in from National Cash Register. It was to start out in Dayton, Ohio, where Wop had been offered some advanced training on special equipment for the company. So in the summer of 1925 the young couple packed their bags and headed off to Ohio.

As Wop worked on a lathe one afternoon, a steel splinter shot up into his right eye. He reeled with pain. When he was rushed to the hospital, a medical team was able to extract the small piece of offending metal from his eye. It looked hopeful that the eye would recover fully from the attack. But it soon became apparent that the damage would be permanent.

Accepting that reality was difficult for the flyer who dreamed more and more of returning to his first and only true vocation. Being grounded for the rest of his life was simply not an option. By now, both Wop and Vi knew that, with both eyes or with only one, Wop would be up in the sky again. It was only a matter of time.

Vi Bode on her horse. Edmonton, 1924.

# 6

# Missions *of* Mercy

Transferred back to Edmonton with NCR in the spring of l926, both Wop and Vi set about re-establishing themselves as a married couple. Vi continued to be in demand to train and show top horses for judging and breeding. With a lot of hard work she won a position once again with the Canadian Women's Polo Team which would be ready by the next year to go into international competition in New York. The team was good enough to bring home the second place trophy.

Wop spent as many of his off hours as possible in the air, flying new aircraft and teaching aspiring young pilots to fly.

It was not long before Wop and his flying friends saw the need for Edmonton to have a full-fledged aerodrome. They plunged themselves into the work to get one and, by the fall of l927, they had it. Blatchford Field became the first municipal aerodrome in Canada complete with a two-plane hangar, thirty-four acres for landing, and funding for runway construction. They had created the forerunner to the modern airport. With an official aerodrome as home base, the flyers could now inaugurate the Edmonton and Northern Alberta Aero Club. The first item of business was to elect a slate of officers. Wop was their choice for First President and Chief Pilot of its pilot training department.

The club of flyers quickly became a closely bonded group of men who were both exhilarated by the freedom from their earthly chains and deeply moved by the uncertainty and fragility of that freedom. When a member of the club crashed, the brothers paid their final tribute with wings and hearts. They would provide the funeral procession with an aerial escort and drop flowers as they circled the grave in a final salute.

In December, NCR announced its move to Calgary. Wop knew a momentary sense of futility. Had he worked to gain all this only to have to leave it behind? It would be six months before he could get a leave of absence

Mercy flight, Edmonton to Fort Vermilion, Jan 2-6 1929. Wop May and Vic Horner receive the serum from Dr Malcolm Bow in Edmonton, January 2 1929.

# *High Hopes Are Held Out for Safety of the Fliers; Cold Weather Against Them*

from the company to return to Edmonton to see to his duties with the Aero Club. When the club decided to make itself a professional training centre, Wop himself went to Moose Jaw to take the course so he could become the pilot trainer.

In so doing he had to announce his resignation from NCR and with that move, his brief interim on the ground was officially over. Airborne he was, airborne he would remain.

As if to underline that pledge made to himself, Wop set new aviation records in altitude and speed within the next few months. He and his friend Blake Dagg achieved an official record when they climbed to a height of 10,000 feet on November 24, 1928.

## A Call for Help

There were other matters as well for a flyer to attend to. Diphtheria, for one. On January 2, 1929, when Wop decided to tackle the unknown and the elements to deliver a

life-saving serum six hundred miles away, he would be transforming aviation from a daring idea to a lifeline.

DIPHTHERIA. FEAR EPIDEMIC. SEND ANTI-TOXIN.

The telegram was short but clear. It had been written by Dr. Harold A. Hamman in Little Red River on December 18, after the Hudson Bay Company manager and his wife became sick with diphtheria. The doctor had very little serum for them and what he had he knew was out-dated and not effective to cure an outbreak in the community. With no way to send a message for help at his disposal, he had made the long trip to Fort Vermilion himself where he hoped to convince the only two men with a horse and sleigh to take his message to the nearest telegraph office, 280 miles to the south at Peace River. The men, William Lambert and Joe Lafleur, agreed to make the trip and arrived with their urgent request for serum twelve days later. It was telegraphed to Edmonton immediately, and received by Alberta's Deputy Health Minister, Dr.M.R. Bow, on New Year's Day.

> Edmonton, Alta. Jan. 3 (A.P.)-An airplane was headed into the north today carrying a supply of antitoxin to two diphtheria-stricken trading posts 600 miles away in the frozen wilderness. Captain Wop May, former Canadian Army pilot, with Vic Horner as passenger, took off yesterday with 500,000 units of antitoxin in response to an appeal for help from settlements at Fort Vermilion and Little Red River. They faced the task of locating the posts in the snow covered forests and landing where no plane has been known to have flown before.
>
> The appeal for antitoxin sent out by Dr. H.A. Hamman, provincial health officer in the north, arrived New Year's Day, dated Dec. 18, and had been brought 167 miles by dog sled to the nearest telegraph office at Peace River. Dr. Hamman said the factor in charge of the Hudson's Bay Company post at Vermilion River had died of diphtheria and an epidemic was feared among the 200 inhabitants of the two posts.

# *Tiny Aeroplane In Race Against Death To North*

41

Mercy Flight to Fort Vermilion. Dr Harold Hamman, Vic Horner, Wop May and the Avro Avian. Fort Vermilion, Jan 3, 1929.

Mercy flight. Preparing aircraft for flight at Peace River, January 6, 1929.

Getting the serum was no problem. Delivering it was quite another matter. Diphtheria could kill an entire community before the serum could get there by dogsled. Bow, like most Albertans, was accustomed to opening the evening paper and finding the face of Wop May staring back at him. Like most, he never tired of reading about the flying adventures of this man. He knew there was only one way that the serum could reach the northern community in time to save the lives of its residents. He knew there were planes available at the Aerodrome. But how could he ask someone to take such a risk?

Mercy flight. Vic Horner & Wop May in the Avro Avian in Edmonton.

Mercy flight, return to Edmonton, January 6, 1929. Mrs Lee, Babe Horner, Mrs May, Vic Horner, Vi May, Wop May.

There was never a question in Wop's mind. It needed to be done. He called his friend Vic Horner, whose ability and companionship he could count on for such a mission. They met Dr. Bow at the Aerodrome and received a package wrapped up in a woollen blanket. It was the serum. They were instructed to keep it warm at all costs which they well knew would be difficult to do in the light, linen-covered Avro. With its open cockpit offering the two pilots no protection, how could they keep their precious cargo warm? They decided to try to set up a charcoal burner in the baggage compartment just behind the cockpit, reachable only from the ground. Unfortunately, this would not provide them with the solution they needed as the burner started to smolder enroute, forcing them to land to put out the fire. By the end of their journey the serum would arrive warm, as per doctor's orders, but the warmth would come from the heat of their own bodies.

Landing gear was another concern as the pilots prepared for their flight. The Avro's wheels were not suitable for landing in deep snow but there were no skis available and no time to wait for a pair. They decided to follow the river and land on the solid ice.

They filled the gas tank with twenty gallons and stored an extra eight for the flight to Peace River. Bundling up into their layers of sweaters, scarves, and the traditional flyers'

**44**

# THE GIANTS

This Episode: Wilfred "Wop" May

AFTER THE WAR, "WOP" MAY STARTS AN AVIATION COMPANY, OPENING CANADA'S *NORTHWEST*, WHERE ONCE ONLY DOGSLEDS OR CANOES COULD VENTURE.

WALT McDAYTER NORMAN DREW

NEW YEAR'S DAY, 1929, IN EDMONTON HE AND PARTNER VIC HORNER HEAR A PLEA...

DIPTHERIA HAS HIT FORT VERMILION! CAN YOU FLY THIS *SERUM* TO THEM?

10-20

THERE'S A BLIZZARD... 400 MILES IN AN *OPEN-COCKPIT* PLANE, IN 50-DEGREES-BELOW... AND WITH NO SKIS TO LAND IN THE SNOW. IMPOSSIBLE..!

IMPOSSIBLE... BUT WE'LL *TRY*. LET'S GO, VIC!

AVRO AVIAN

McDayter and Drew, Calgary *Herald*, October 1965.

caps with earflaps, they climbed aboard their 75-horsepower Avro Avian, one in each cockpit. They tested the dual controls, checked the map and compass. Then Wop gave the high sign to the field mechanic to start the propeller. As the engine roared to life, Vi ran over to the plane and handed Wop some chocolate bars. He smiled down at her. As always she said good-bye with a wave, not a tear, for she knew he had to go. He would always have to go. She waved until the aircraft became a tiny winged speck.

Over the next hours, all of the combined skill and strength of both men would be required to hold the plane to the course Wop had mapped out. They tried not to think how slim their chances really were as the wind opposed them relentlessly and the snow hit their faces in icy chunks at the 500-foot altitude. With visibility almost nil, they were grateful when the storm finally subsided enough to show them some ground and they could re-establish their position.

Little did the two flyers realize in the blinding fury around them that their flight was attracting a great deal of attention all over the country as well as on the ground just

below them. Leon Giroux and his friends in McLennan Junction, heard the news through radio broadcasts on their crystal sets. They decided to clear a landing field just in case the two pilots were heading their way on the mercy flight. They marked their clearing with flags and stood watch.

They didn't have long to wait.

At 4:20 that afternoon, flying low over the Edmonton Dunvegan and British Columbia Railway line, Wop caught some activity on the lake below them. He dropped and circled back. Seeing the welcoming field below, the two fliers decided to take advantage of it. Much to the excitement of their "ground crew", and their own relief at finding a place out of the storm for a while, they landed easily on the McLennan Junction runway. They had made 267 miles of the 600-mile trip in four hours, despite the strong headwinds, poor visibility, and a temperature of -30°F.

With the help of their excited hosts, they anchored the plane and drained the oil from its engine. Then they took the oil, their precious cargo of serum, and their frozen bodies into the warmth of the McLennan Junction hospitality.

# *Wop May Back Safe at Peace River*

They were at Peace River for fuelling the next day before noon, once again receiving an enthusiastic welcome from the local residents who were watching for their arrival. Leaving Peace River gave them all an unexpected experience. As the plane lifted off the ice for the last lap of their journey, Wop saw that they couldn't get enough altitude in time to clear the railway bridge over the river. With the Edmonton high level bridge in mind, he made an instant decision and the plane was flying under the bridge, then up and away on the other side, to the cheers of the entire community below them.

Following the river's course, Wop and Vic finally arrived at Fort Vermilion just before dark. As at their two other landing points, this one had been cleared by the residents as they watched the sky anxiously for the sight of the now famous mercy flight.

Harold Hamman, the doctor who had sent the original SOS, recognized courage when he saw it. As he took the serum from Wop and Vic, he marvelled at the spirit of humanity and stamina in two such men whose white, snow-crusted faces showed the strain of the past two days. The doctor didn't stay to join Fort Vermilion's brand of hospitality lavished on the two famous visitors, for the rest of the delivery was now up to him. And off he went, racing his horse and sleigh over the fifty miles back to Little Red River to administer the life-saving serum to its people.

## A Royal Homecoming

The next day, their mission accomplished, Wop and Vic filled up the tank with the only fuel around, car gasoline, turned the faithful Avian south, and headed for home. By the time they had coughed, sputtered, and pushed their way through to Peace River on the car fuel, the plane needed major engine work. The pilots also needed major repairs. They had to be helped from the plane, so frozen and numbed were they from sitting in the minus 33°F temperature at the mercy of the cold, driving wind. But they were in good hands in this small community, good warm hands that were now an essential part of this entire mission of mercy. Once more they thawed out and revived, and, once their engine was in working order, they were on their way again, eager to be home.

Poor visibility kept them at one hundred feet for most of the distance into Edmonton. The goggles helped keep their eyelashes from freezing so that their vision was not impaired, a major consideration particularly to Wop, whose vision at the best of times came from only one eye. There was no such protection against the bitter cold for their mouths and noses, however, and by the end of the trip they had large sore blisters on their faces which would be a long time in healing, and never forgotten.

But they were heading home, and by 3 o'clock on Sunday afternoon Wop had executed a perfect landing onto the Edmonton field, where they discovered they were to be the guests of honour at a landing party.

Edmonton was welcoming its heroes home in style. Hardly had the Avian's belaboured propeller made its final revolution when a surge of cheering people mounted the weary flyers to their shoulders and carried them to the shelter of the hangar. Speeches, sirens, flashing lights, and a royal procession through the middle of the city were reported in newspapers around the country. As for the flyers and their families, they were grateful for a successful mission, a safe return, and the warmth of home.

Besides the banner headlines, the detailed accounts of every mile of the journey, and the pictures of the pilots with which the press covered its pages, an editorial was written to praise the special brand of courage shown by Wop May and Vic Horner. It was entitled "What price human life?" and had particular implications for Wop's continuing interest in establishing northern air transportation.

> With the lives of five hundred persons at a wilderness post as the stake, the government of Alberta should not gamble everything on the audacious courage of two Edmonton flyers and the airworthiness of a tiny Avian plane. A second plane should be dispatched at once to act as a reserve to that one supposedly winging its way over the uninhabited stretch of coun-

> try between Peace River and Fort Vermilion.

> In other parts of Canada where rescue or relief planes have been sent into isolated country, two planes have been used. It is below zero weather in the north today and the plane used by Capt. May and Vic Horner has no enclosed cabin. The threat of snow adds to the difficulties of flight over the wilderness. If the plane is forced down in the wilderness it will be days, even weeks, before news can reach the outside. Even if the flyers reach Fort Vermilion today, Edmonton cannot know it for nearly two weeks and in the meantime the authorities' hands are tied by ignorance of what has happened.

> Precious hours already have been lost in getting a second plane ready to follow the trail of the first. The provincial and federal governments ought to cooperate at once to ensure the dispatch of the reserve plane, either from High River or from the Winnipeg hangar of the Western Canada Airways. The provincial government deserves every credit for what it has already done, but if anything should happen to May and Horner, the people of Alberta will hold the government to blame for a blot on the escutcheon of the province caused by a willingness to gamble with human life instead of incurring the expense required to lessen the hazards of the flight of mercy.

A re-enactment of the mercy flight from Edmonton to Fort Vermilion, fifty years later, by Bob Horner and Denny May, sons of the original pilots. June 21,1979.

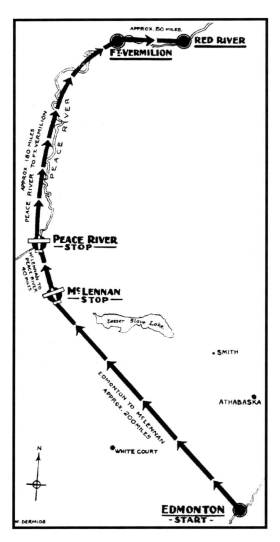

## The Mission Remembered

On June 21, 1979, a commemorative flight was organized by the Lutheran Association of Missionaries and Pilots (LAMP) to celebrate the Fiftieth Anniversary of the mission of mercy. The money raised by the flight was enough to purchase a new Cessna 185 for missionary work of Pastor Pilots. The sons of the two flyers, Denny May and Bob Horner, occupied the two seats in the open cockpit of the 1930 plane shined up for the occasion. Both of the doctors who had participated in the original mercy flight were on hand to perform their original roles in the re-enactment. Dr. M.R. Bow, at 92, presented the serum to the flyers in a blanket in Edmonton, and Dr. Harold A. Hamman received it at Fort Vermilion.

Waving goodbye, as always, was Vi May, a flood of memories filling her, stripping away the fifty years in between to allow her a full view of that bitter cold January day when she had waved goodbye to a moth in a snowstorm.

Wop's son Denny, for whom this was a highly emotional experience connecting him intensely with the father he had lost at the age of seventeen, described the flight:

Dr. Malcolm Bow and Vi May wave goodbye to Denny in the Fleet Finch at the 50th Anniversary re-enactment of the 1929 Mercy Flight. June 21, 1979.

It's so noisy you can't hear a thing. Wop and Vic wouldn't have said too much to each other enroute. And cold, even in June with parkas over our flight suits it was cold.

How much colder it would have been for them in the January temperatures of thirty below, especially in a blizzard! Perishing conditions, and they both knew that. There's just nothing to stop the wind and the cold in an open cockpit, made even colder at such an altitude at such a speed. Yet it is the most exhilarating feeling in the whole world to be in the air close enough to the ground to wave at a schoolyard full of kids and to see wildlife at such a close range. We were free

to enjoy our trip. We didn't have their worries. We had fuel stops scheduled along the way with lots of good airplane gasoline. They had to use whatever gasoline they could scrounge, most of it was automobile gas which plugged the airplane's engine system.

The participants in the commemorative flight discovered people along the way who had helped Wop and Vic in landing, or fuelling, or thawing out, and who remembered. Some travelled many miles to be in Fort Vermilion to mark the occasion, grateful to be alive because of the efforts of two courageous flyers, fifty years before.

# 7

# To Hollywood
# *and* Back Again

Photo showing crashed Sopwith Camel on the movie set of *Hell's Angels*, Los Angeles, California, 1927. Inscribed by stuntman named Robbie.

Commercial Airways President Cy Becker came up with the next job for the famous pair of flyers. This time, Wop and Vic were to go south, all the way to California, to pick up an all-metal monoplane. The Lockheed Vega had a major advantage for Becker's plans for the company. It could be fitted with skis or wheels and changed for the seasons, an important feature now that flying had been established as a year-round possibility. Becker had made the deal with Howard Hughes, who owned the Lockheed Manufacturing Company.

The reputation of the two Canadian flyers preceded them. And when the call went out for help with some real flying shots in Hughes' latest movie *Hell's Angels*, the Canadians came to the rescue.

Wop kept a memento of that trip. It was a photograph showing the scene of an air crash from the film. On the picture was an inscription written by the movie's stuntman. It read: "Wop. If I had known as much about these crates as you, I would never have stacked."

*Hell's Angels* got its authentic flying shots while Wop and Vic got enough of the movie-making world to last them a lifetime. They much preferred the adventures in the real world, and, as it happened, the Vega would figure prominently in many of them.

## The Orange Cigar

On May 24 and 25, 1929, Wop put the Vega into action to set two new aviation records. The big Winnipeg Air Show was the second annual exhibition for the newly formed Winnipeg Flying Club. Pilots from all over North America would be there and Wop was keen to attend. He boarded the Vega and headed east. By the time he landed in Winnipeg, six hours later, he had set two new

Wop May and Vic Horner with the two Commercial Airways Aircraft, the Avro Avian and the Lockheed Vega. Edmonton, 1927.

Vic Horner and Wop May receive the Lockheed Vega in California, 1929.

aviation records, one for speed and the other for the first non-stop flight between the two cities. He also would win second prize for aerobatics in a borrowed aircraft during the show itself.

On September 6, Wop took on the fastest train in northern Alberta to race their delivery of newspapers. By the time the train reached its destination, Wop had delivered his papers, staged an aerial exhibition above the train, and returned home. His speed was clocked at 150 miles an hour.

The Vega , fondly referred to now as The Orange Cigar, and its famous pilot also became a welcome sight as they answered calls for help. Once, it was a diphtheria outbreak in a small town marooned by snow-blocked roads,

requiring an anti-toxin plus a nurse. Another time, an oxygen tank wrapped in rubber tubes was flown and dropped from a low altitude at stalling speed to save the life of a farmer dying of pneumonia in Fairview, 450 miles northwest of Edmonton. Later, food was the package when Wop made a rescue flight to the Peace River District where 120 people became stranded by late spring rains in their trek north to establish a new settlement.

All in all, it was enough business to make Commercial Airways' Cy Becker listen to Wop's proposal of opening up a northern airbase. Wop had his eye on the perfect place. The end of steel. Fort McMurray.

Vic Horner and Wop May bring the Lockheed Vega to Edmonton, 1929.

Wop May with the Bellanca CH-300 Pacemaker, Edmonton , 1929.

# 8

## *The* Mays *of* Fort McMurray

**Vi May and son Denny - May 1935.**

By late l929, Fort McMurray was a bustling town of 750 permanent residents, with a hotel, drugstore, telegraph office, general store, meat market, confectionery, and a community hall. Due to its strategic location on a rail line and a major river, it was the connecting link between north and south. It would continue to grow in size and importance into what is known today as the regional city of Wood Buffalo.

The first time he landed in the town, Wop could see the possibilities. It was at the junction of the Athabasca and Clearwater rivers, but there was a large protected area of smooth ice, laid out for him like a welcome mat, not the rough ice that normally freezes on a river with a strong current. What he had discovered and would later utilize was The Snye, a backwater part of the river forming a natural reservoir, protected from wind and current. His pilot's eye could see where he could erect a nose hangar for engine maintenance...to service a northern cargo route...to take the supplies that came from Edmonton on the rail line into the far northern reaches...

All this was enough to convince Cy Becker that Fort McMurray would serve his company well as a northern airbase if he could talk Wop May into coming to work for him. He trusted Wop's visionary instincts as much as his flying skills.

## The Newcomers Move In

It didn't take much for Wop to persuade Vi to make the move. Despite her genteel ways and her very proper British accent, and despite her involvement in the equestrian community in Edmonton, she was every bit as adventurous as her flying husband. Moving to Fort McMurray from the established traditions of the more settled area of southern Alberta simply gave her a broader base for her natural curiosity and inventiveness.

A thirty-six-hour train ride with their household goods started the move off for Vi. The train would go a few miles and then stop. Go a few more and stop again. When Vi decided to investigate and see what the trouble was, she was told that there was no trouble. The engineer happened to be a trapper and he was merely checking his traplines along the way!

When she finally arrived at her destination, Vi's first priority was to create a home for Wop and herself. The structure provided was a small frame building on the main street that still resembled the barber shop it had once been, with its high square front façade. To make it into suitable living quarters, they divided it up into three rooms, front, centre, and back.

Keeping it warm provided the first major challenge. Despite a heater between the front and middle rooms and the stove in the kitchen, the winter brought a layer of ice to the inside walls. The resourceful lady of the house solved the problem by hanging blankets on the walls, serving both to decorate and warm the interior. The blankets cooperated:

Alex and Elizabeth May, Wop's parents visit Fort McMurray.

they kept in place by quickly freezing to the walls, and there they stayed until the advent of spring.

Together, the Mays created the centrepiece for their home – a kitchen table-bathtub – which became the envy of the neighbourhood. For meals it served as a long white enamel table, adaptable to whatever number of guests happened along. On bath nights it was cleared off and turned on its side, revealing Wop's inventive genius – a deep tub and a hose pipe complete with plug, easily filled, easily emptied. Their modern

Franklin Avenue looking west.

conveniences of bathing, cooking, and heating were dependent on the weekly delivery of wood, coal, and water which in turn depended on manpower and weather conditions.

With her warm and outgoing manner, Vi was not long in making friends, which left her little time to be lonesome during the long waits for her husband. In particular, she was not long in discovering the kindred spirit of Gladys Hill, who like Vi, had been born in England. Gladys had made history in the town in 1923 when she arrived, for she had been its first white woman. She had continued her firsts by becoming the first female town councillor and, in the fifties, by serving as acting mayor. Like Vi, Gladys was also married to a man who was gone for weeks at a time. When he was in town he served as the pharmacist, vet, doctor, and dentist; but he also transported supplies from one settlement

to another. Not in the air like Wop, but by dogsled.

Left to tend the home fires for long stretches of time, Vi and Gladys spent a lot of time together and enjoyed each other's company. They discovered a mutual love of fishing, swimming, and hunting. In the evenings, they enjoyed listening to the opera on the Atwater-Kent radio set that Wop had specially rigged up. Rabbit and grouse were often on the menu at both households thanks to a unique kind of teamwork established by the two women. Although Vi could bring down her own game single-handedly, when she was with Gladys, she was the eyes, and Gladys the shot. Vi would spot and point. Gladys would aim and fire.

Together they also made social events happen in Fort McMurray. Tennis tournaments, cycling excursions on the flats, and picnics were favourite summer outings. When they planned dances, everyone came from miles around, trappers, miners, Indians, children. They came by boat, plane, and dogsled for the occasion.

Vi had to organize one of the largest social events without Gladys. Fire had broken out in the town's saloon. It had swept through the grocery and butcher shops, and hadn't stopped until it had levelled most of one side of the main street. This included the Walter Hill Drugstore. With Walter away, Gladys had managed to save her son and herself and had then gone back to get the ledgers, prescription file, and the money. Vi got no opposition from anyone in town when she decided to organize a surprise fire social for those families who had lost so much, including her dear friend Gladys. The social was a success. The town rebuilt itself and carried on.

Often, with Wop away and Gladys busy elsewhere, Vi would set out on her own along the swift-flowing Athabasca in a small boat with a motor. It was a busy river route with a variety of traffic to stir her curiosity. She was able to fill her diary with parades of tugs and steamboats and the trappers who built the woodpiles along the way to fuel them. She would steer herself along the shoreline, fascinated by the black, oily muck oozing out of the riverbank. She was a familiar figure to the Chipewyan Indians who also travelled the river, and she would stop and visit with them in their camps.

On one such excursion, the current carried her far beyond any hope of returning home by nightfall. Far beyond where she had gone before. When she spotted the smoke from a cabin she brought her boat onto the bank, relieved to find some signs of human habitation at such a late hour. To her surprise she was not greeted but rather growled at by an old trapper. Unlike most of the trappers she knew, he did not seem to welcome guests at any hour. It took considerable negotiating before Vi was given a piece of floor at the far corner of his cabin to sleep. She spent a disturbing night with the cabin's mouse population running over her face with their sticky feet. At daybreak the next morning she made a swift and silent departure.

As the air business boomed and freight hauls grew into passenger loads, the Mays had frequent house guests. Vi never knew whether she'd be feeding a mining prospector with a load of gold from the Athabasca gold field, packing a lunch for a north-bound fur trapper and his team of dogs, or preparing a nursing station for an injured Inuit brought back from the Aklavik run by Wop. No matter who they were, or how many of them there were, they were all greeted equally once they arrived at the May residence. Everyone was given a job to do. Everyone had lots to eat, which usually included at least three desserts. After dinner there were the pranks, equally played on everyone. These were Wop's department. City friends were usually initiated to the north by being locked in the outhouse, or by being admitted into one of Wop's many betting games.

One of their most frequent guests was Tim Sims. Officially, he was a service rep for Wright engines in Canada and had legitimate reasons for frequent visits to the country's busiest northern airbase. Unofficially, he found Vi to be the best hostess of all his service stops, and Wop to be always fit, vigorous, and ready for some action, such as getting someone to bet money on how many drops were left in an empty liquor bottle. Many an overnight guest would go to bed smiling at the victory of calling the last drop, only to be awakened before daybreak to be told they owed Wop a case of scotch. He had sat up for the final drop.

## The Bellanca Wins

Having proved its success in the northern transportation business, Commercial Airways got the financing it needed from the brokerage firm of Solloway Mills, and Wop headed to Montreal to buy planes. A happy task for a born flyer building an air route. As far as he was concerned there were only two companies in the running for his business, the Fairchilds and the Bellancas. The Fairchilds showed him their best, the Wasp-powered Super Universal and the Wasp Fairchild 71. The Bellancas had only one model, the relatively new Bellanca with the Wright J6 engine. He chose the Bellanca and bought three of them.

The Fairchilds were not good losers. Unhappy at failing to get the sale, they wired Solloway Mills to report that the chief pilot for Commercial Airways had been carousing since his arrival in Montreal. Solloway, however, knew their man better than that and threw the cable in the garbage.

At Wop's request, Tim Sims became part of the Bellanca deal as the mechanic for the flight home. It turned out to be a four-day flight back with stops at Sault Ste Marie, Sioux Lookout and Berens River. At Winnipeg they met up with Leigh Brintnell of Western Canada Airways, chief competitor to Commercial Airways at that time. Brintnell's comment as he checked Wop's new machine was that it wouldn't stand up to the job like the Super Universals that Western used. Wop chose not to make a comeback at that point. After all, the Bellanca was so new it didn't have a track record of any kind. However, heading north out of Edmonton on the last leg of their trip, they joined up with a Western plane and flew with it for a few miles. Finally Wop looked across at Sims with a gleam in his eye that was quite familiar to his friend by now. The Wop May gambler's glint. Wop made the move and the Bellanca pulled smoothly ahead, leaving the Western plane far behind. Wop had made the right choice after all.

# 9

# *A* Mail Route *to* Aklavik

First air-mail flight, Fort McMurray to Aklavik 1929/30.

Aklavik!

Winning the contract to take the mail to Aklavik took Wop's imagination beyond the frontier of man's knowledge. Beyond the northern reaches of the north. Beyond civilization. He had taken out a map to have a look at it. There it was...close to the Yukon and Northwest Territories borders, inside the Arctic Circle...just past Fort McPherson on a tributary of the MacKenzie, right at the mouth... If one were to follow the river...

But then another thought took shape in his mind. If one were to follow the Athabasca up to Fort Chipewyan, hit Fitzgerald, Smith, Resolution, then cut across Great Slave Lake about there...to Providence and up the Mackenzie to...Simpson...and Norman...with fuel caches maybe here...and there...and there... Why, there would be no reason not to deliver mail to everyone along the river. It could be a mail route! A flying mail route with service within hours instead of weeks.

Wop was particularly keen to tell his father. Alex May, as Postmaster, in Edmonton had been part of the historic occasion that had initiated the city's first organized letter carriers on June 1, 1907, making Edmonton the first city between Vancouver and Winnipeg with door to door postal delivery. Now his son, twenty-two years later, would take the mail by air to Aklavik and begin a northern mail route.

In no time, the development was being heralded as the start of the peaceful revolution of the Canadian North. Mercy flights were one thing; regular service routes were quite another. Service meant settlement, development, people, business. With service as far north as the Mackenzie Delta, the extension of civilization would reach beyond the Arctic Circle.

Aklavik!

# Commercial Airways Limited

HEAD OFFICE: EDMONTON

*BASES SHOWN ON MAP LEGEND*

Edmonton, Alta. PHONE **1551**

Edmonton, Alta. PHONE **1551**

# MACKENZIE RIVER DISTRICT

### RATES

**From Fort McMurray To—**

| To— | Passenger | Express Per Lb. |
|---|---|---|
| Fort Chipewyan | $ 35.00 | $ .20 |
| Fort Fitzgerald | 65.00 | .35 |
| Fort Smith | 65.00 | .35 |
| Fort Resolution | 100.00 | .70 |
| Hay River | 135.00 | .75 |
| Fort Providence | 160.00 | .85 |
| Fort Simpson | 205 00 | 1.00 |
| Fort Wrigley | 240.00 | 1.3 |
| Fort Norman | 280.00 | 1.65 |
| Good Hope | 325 00 | 2.15 |
| Arctic Red River | 375.00 | 2.50 |
| Fort McPherson | 390.00 | 2.60 |
| Aklavik | 410.00 | 2.70 |

The above are the rates for ordinary schedule flights on the route mentioned.

Special flights may be arranged for.

Each passenger is entitled to carry 25 lbs. of baggage free, all in excess of that weight charged accordingly.

All traffic rates listed above are subject to change without notice.

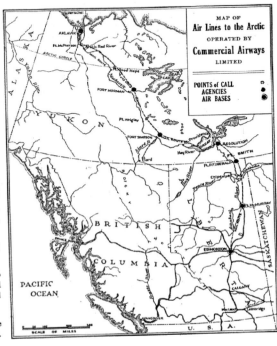

MAP OF
Air Lines to the Arctic
OPERATED BY
**Commercial Airways**
LIMITED

POINTS of CALL
AGENCIES
AIR BASES

### WINTER SCHEDULE 1929 - 1930

**NORTH-BOUND**

**Leave Fort McMurray**
**For Fort Resolution:**
Nov. 27;  Dec. 4, 11, 18, 25;
Jan. 1, 8, 15, 22, 29;
Feb. 5, 12, 19, 26;
Mar. 5, 12, 19, 26;  Apr. 2, 9.
**For Fort Simpson:**
Nov. 27;  Dec. 25;  Jan. 22;
Feb. 12;  Mar. 5, 26.
**For Aklavik:**
Nov. 27;  Jan. 22;  Mar. 26.

**SOUTH-BOUND**

**Leave Aklavik:**
Dec. 3;  Feb. 28;  Apr. 1.
**Leave Fort Simpson:**
Dec. 5, 28;  Jan. 28;  Feb. 15;
Mar. 8;  Apr. 3.
**Leave Fort Resolution:**
Nov. 29;  Dec. 6, 13, 20, 28;
Jan. 3, 10, 17, 24;
Feb. 1, 7, 15, 21, 28;
Mar. 8, 14, 21, 28;  Apr. 4, 11.

On the above flights, the aircraft will stop at intermediate posts.

The schedule is tentative, and rigid adherence to it will depend upon weather.

## SHIPPING INSTRUCTIONS:

Mark North-bound Parcels care of "COMMERCIAL AIRWAYS LIMITED, FORT McMURRAY, Alberta," via Northern Alberta Railways' Express—"Air charges COLLECT" or "PREPAID."

Shippers are required to prepay Railway Express Charges to Fort McMurray on North Bound Traffic.

EXAMPLE:

| | |
|---|---|
| *From* | JOHN DOE, 411 - 81st Ave., Edmonton, Alta. |
| *To* | JAS. SMITH, Ft. Resolution, N.W.T., c/o Commercial Airways Ltd., Ft. McMurray, Alta. |

Via N. A. R. Express.  "Air Charges Collect" (or otherwise)

Pack parcels securely. Parcels must be kept within the following limit (outside measurements)
12-in. x 20-in. x 60-in.

Add 2-in. to width for each decrease of 12-in. in length.

C. BECKER, General Manager.

Poster showing route and rates for shipping packages north. Commercial Airways, 1929-30.

L-R: Frank Welborne, Postmaster
Guy Rocke, Pilot Wop May with mail
on sled.

With a full surge of pride and exuberance, Wop lifted the orange Bellanca flagship bearing the Royal Mail cipher on each side. He looked around to make sure the other two Bellancas and the Vega were up and flying with him. A flying flotilla. As he tracked each plane, he reviewed the crew he would be flying with for the next few days. There was Cy Becker himself, a flyer as well as the manager of Commercial Airways. The Brit on board, flyer "Boom" Lumsden, had learned his flying with the RAF but couldn't resist the lure of the fishing tales coming out of Canada. Moss Burbidge was one of the finest flying instructors in the country, but, as everyone knew, he would be in a hurry to get back to civilization.

Then there was the Black Gang. The mechanics, a hand-picked crew for this job. As Wop and the other pilots well knew, it would be the Black Gang who made the real difference on this long cold flight. Casey VanderLinden from Holland could be counted on to be cheerful and had an obsession for a smooth-running engine even at sixty degrees below zero. Stan Green had come highly recommended although Wop didn't know him too well at this point. Archie McMullen was an engineer who could make it to pilot if he wanted, as was Don Robertson from England, a rookie but a fast learner. Then there were the two "civilians", Postal Inspector Walter Hale, who had wanted badly to be a part of this historic flight, and *Edmonton Journal* reporter Ted Watt. Although they didn't bring any aviation expertise with them, Wop had noticed that they both pitched in with the loading and the fuelling of the planes. All in all a full crew that carried a full load: five tons of mail, 125,000 letters, over a distance of 1800 miles.

## Charting the Future

The flat bush land below them was strewn with lakes and rivers that wore their winter coat of snow and ice. After the bitter cold of his flight with Vic Horner a year earlier, Wop was grateful for the improvements Vi had made to his outer garments. The duffel linings

Transferring mail from plant to dog train at Fort Smith, at -52°F.

she had sewn into his parka, mitts and mukluks had already made a difference. The woollen lining kept his body heat in where he needed it while the canvas material outside kept the wind away and was less bulky for getting in and out of the plane. He particularly welcomed the wolf fur trim of the hood because it wouldn't freeze. He had had enough of freezing.

As they travelled further north, the trees grew smaller, giving way to rocks and snow-swept lakes. The sun chased shadows on the swoops and swells, and the vast pristine world was marked only by the creatures who lived there. Wop was well aware that with

Arrival of the aircraft at Fort Resolution.

Arrival in Aklavik - local people meet the aircraft.

this trip he would be discovering things about this country that had never been known before. He would be flying over areas not marked on any map. He would have to learn what a plane could do and should do in this cold; what a pilot had to do to keep his plane flying and himself alive; how a plane could be landed when there was no place to land. He would have to learn what to do in an emergency and then do everything not to have it happen. From now on, his ventures into the north would not be single, occasional rescue flights. On those he had been lucky so far, but now he would have to learn and learn well how to do the job of flying regularly in the north. The future would depend on it.

At Fort Smith, Wop turned off the engine and stepped out of the Bellanca, stretching his cramped legs. They'd be two planes less after this stop. One, in fact, had already headed back south, its load delivered. The planes had barely landed when the townspeople gathered around them, excited and hospitable. Talk

and food sounded good to the weary travellers, but they would have to wait until they had bedded down their faithful machines.

With the help of their welcoming committee, they chopped holes in the ice. The next step in the procedure was watched in amazement as the pilots and their mechanics put gasoline, a lighted match, and an end of rope from a plane into each hole. As the flames melted the ice and then the water quickly froze around the rope ends, the anchor that had been made would hold the planes solidly in position. Next they drained the oil from the engines and covered the motors with large canvas and asbestos blankets.

By the next morning the people of Fort Smith could understand the importance of the mooring procedure. During the night the wind had blown high drifts around the planes but had not been able to do them any damage. They had remained securely fastened. Wop and his crew warmed the oil as the townspeople cleared the snow away from the planes. Then, fuelled and ready, the signals were given to turn the propellers and everyone felt the reward of their efforts as the motors roared to life. The ice and snow were removed from the wings and the moorings untied. Only one job was left to do, and that was for the pilots to pack themselves a runway. They taxied up and down the snow-drifted ice, letting the skis do the packing. And then they were up once more.

From here on they were entering the unchartered part of the journey, the section of the country cut off from communication with the outside world except for two mail deliveries a year. The day lay bright and clear for this new landscape. Wop climbed to 10,000 feet and was rewarded with a vista of fifty miles on all sides. The further north he flew along the Mackenzie, the more the daylight became only a promise and a glow from the southern sun. He knew that on a summer's flight however, the vista would not be ended by a night sky, for at that time of year this country became the land of the midnight sun.

On the snow-covered flatlands below him grazed a large herd of caribou. He resisted an urge to come lower to get a better view, but some miles further along he made a different decision as he spotted another herd, galloping this time. He dipped low to join their wild charge across the flat, white stretch of land, marvelling at their graceful power.

Every once in awhile the Mackenzie opened up in a series of rapids with the frosty vapour rising up into the frigid air.

The Hudson's Bay Company (HBC) outposts stretching along the river became a welcome sight for the pilot of the flagship. The first sign was usually the bright red HBC ensign flying high on a flagpole. This identified a cluster of mud and log buildings in a clearing, the gathering place for hunters, trappers, miners, Indians, and missionaries. Before the engine had come to a full stop, a line of parka-wrapped men reached the door of the plane to greet the new arrivals. Many hands sorted the eagerly awaited mail and other supplies, while others helped the pilots and their mechanics bed down their planes for the night.

Then, with the work done, the hospitality began in a mixed medley of Chipewyan, English, and French, with the guests of honour being royally treated to stewed skunk and homebrew, or whatever was on tap. Nights were spent in their own eiderdown sleeping bags on church pews, on the floors of abandoned shacks, or in their own flying machines.

## A Christmas Feast

By Christmas Day, they had reached Fort Good Hope. It had been an exciting and successful trip so far, but Wop and his crew were miles away from home and feeling the effects of the long trip. As Wop looked around at the others, he saw the same thoughts reflected in their long and grizzled faces. Obviously, they all needed something special to celebrate this day.

Wop disappeared into the cockpit of his plane and suddenly all sorts of packages were flying out onto the snow. Turkey. Black rum. Vi's Christmas cake. The makings of a Christmas feast. All they had to do was find

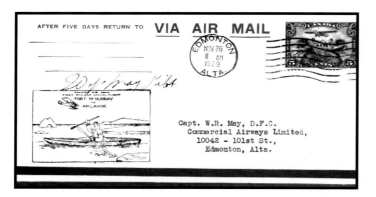

Airmail covers from the first flight — one of 6 autographed by Glynn Roberts (pilot CF-AJR), Wop May (pilot CF-AKI), Tim Sims (Engineer Wright Engines), Casey Van Der Linden (mechanic), Walter Hale (Postal Inspector).

some shelter for the night. With so much at stake, the crew quickly commandeered an abandoned log shack and got a fire going in the woodstove. In went the turkey, all twenty frozen pounds of it. Out came the rum bottle to a loud cheer. The bottle was opened, saluted, and tipped. But not a drop would flow from its slender neck. Frozen solid.

They looked at the fire. Too chancy to throw the bottle in with the turkey. But thirst provides a mighty motive for ingenuity, and the crew was up to it as all pitched in to get the rum to move out of that bottle.

By this time, the noise from the cabin had raised the curiosity of the natives who generously supplied the Fort Good Hope version of Christmas cheer until the rum was thawed. And, as they smelled the cooking turkey, they sat around telling their tales of the Thunderbird, wilderness bravery, and polar buccaneers.

Wop's stomach eventually got the better of his imagination, and he pulled the turkey out of the stove. Black and burnt enough on the outside it was, but still frozen in the centre. Grabbing an axe, he instructed his crew to collect enough snow to fill all available pans and they would go for turkey stew.

A little later, as they finished off their Christmas dinner to the howling chorus of the sled dogs nearby, all agreed that it was better by far than stewed skunk and homebrew.

Next morning it was business as usual. The woodstoves were put to work again to heat up the motor oil, gasoline barrels were dug out of the snow and rolled down to the planes for fuelling. A blowtorch was taken — carefully, and always with a fire extinguisher close at hand — to the cylinders to warm them up. Then the scramble to get on board before the engines cooled down and the dangerous warming up procedure had to be repeated. Then they were headed north again, on the last leg of the journey that would end when they reached Aklavik. Noticing the tell-tale frosted willows of a new river ahead, Wop checked his map and found that it was

Return to Edmonton, January 1930. Bellanca aircraft L-R: Ted Watt (Press Reporter), Guy Rocke (Fort McMurray Postmaster) Tim Sims (Wright Engines), Cy Becker (Manager Commercial Airways), Walter Hale (Postal Inspector), F.X.J. Leger (District Postal Superintendent), Wop May (Pilot), I.C. Soloway (Financial Broker).

Rat River, which signalled the start of a continuous line of snow-capped mountain peaks and purple-shadowed valleys. It would be this river and these mountains that would hide a desperate fugitive three years later and bring Wop back into this area on a very different mission.

A quick stop was made at Fort McPherson by the flagship, while the other plane remained airborne to display some aerial curtsies for the settlement down below. And then, what was now left of the flying flotilla was off across the Mackenzie Delta to the final destination, somewhere ahead on a peninsula in the middle of the alluvial fan that marked the Mackenzie's exit out into the Polar Sea...Aklavik!

Dead ahead now. There it was, the capital of the Arctic. The final destination of the world's longest mail route. It had taken two weeks to cover what would take two months by dogsled. A dream had become a reality.

## Meeting the Inuit

Since its establishment in the summer of 1923 as the headquarters for the Hudson's Bay Company and the RCMP, Aklavik had grown in size and importance. It needed a connection with the outside world to service its commerce and its population on a more regular basis than twice a year. The arrival of the mail fleet had been anticipated with high excitement. Although they hadn't known when it was coming, they knew it would be there. Boats had brought fuel for the airplanes all during the previous summer in preparation for the event. Now that it had finally happened, it was an occasion that would be marked with high honour.

Aklavik Postmaster Bishop Geddes officially welcomed the carriers of His Royal Highness's mail, including the Postal Inspector Walter Hale. Then he introduced the Aklavik officials, including Inspector A.E. Eames of the RCMP and Sergeant Earl Hersey

**67**

of the Canadian Army Signal Corps. After that it was every man for himself as the crowd pressed in on the flyers. Traders from all parts of the world, missionaries, and the many different natives themselves.

It was the tall smiling Inuit visitors who arrived from somewhere even farther north who would be the ones to capture Wop's imagination in their hairy caribou parkas.

Supplies were unloaded, and the three-day celebration began. For Wop it meant a chance to study these fascinating northern people. They responded warmly to him and let him into their homes and showed him their ways. He watched the women chewing animal skins to soften them for sewing into mukluks. Puzzled when he saw such incongruous items as a gramophone, a typewriter, a camera, sewing machines, and washing machines in their log igloos, he inquired as to how these modern things had found their way into this place.

Inspector Eames had the answer. It was the reason the RCMP had been called there in the first place. The original white whalers and traders had discovered they could get valuable whales, white fox, seals, and caribou from the natives in exchange for whiskey, firearms, and these modern machines from the white man's world.

With no limitations put on this treasury, the animal population had been almost depleted within a few years. The diseases that accompanied this exchange, such as syphilis, measles, and other highly contagious diseases, decimated the native population as well. They had no way of treating these new sicknesses or of containing their spread. In contrast, the

Inuit to the north only came to visit, and kept more to their traditional ways of life, living off the land.

The last day of the stopover, as the planes were pronounced ready for the long return trip, Wop finally agreed to the clamouring of the natives for a plane ride. He had decided on a short, straight course for them, fearing that they would be nervous once they were airborne. To his complete surprise, they showed no fear whatever. Indeed, they cheered and applauded his every manoeuvre, wanting more.

## Changing to Survive

As time went by and the north claimed his full attention, Wop began to make some important adaptations to his aircraft. As he was Chief Pilot of a fleet of six mail carriers, these changes eventually affected all the aircraft flying into the north. The best wood for skis was found to be ash and hickory, and the pedestals were laminated to give them further strength and durability. Always careful to treat the oil as the precious commodity it was for his engine, Wop enclosed the oil tanks in a felt and canvas jacket to keep them as warm as he was. Large hand-operated draincocks were fitted to the oil tanks so that he could drain the hot oil as soon as the engine stopped. Then he designed special containers to collect the oil so that it could be reheated over a campfire or blowtorch before starting up the engine the next morning.

Some things he learned the hard way. Bungee cords, used to hold the skis in position for landing, become frozen and lose their elasticity when they get wet in the cold spring temperatures. When this happens they cannot hold the skis in the correct position for landing. The first time this happened to Wop, all he had was a hope and a prayer (and his good luck charms) that the cords would dry and function properly before he had to land the plane. Luck was with him that time. But extra bungee cords were packed for the next flight.

He had learned much earlier how to make a base for his plane when he had to make an emergency landing in a tangle of long muskeg weeds. That experience had also made him realize that sometimes he would have to make the necessary repairs to his machine himself. An emergency landing north of Lac La Biche had taught him that sometimes you just had to wait for help, so you had to be ready to wait. The problem then had been that the engine had swallowed one of the valve heads, a job he could not repair himself. As he set up camp to wait for help he realized how lucky he was to be carrying a freight load of frozen chicken, wondering how many ways there were to cook chicken if he wasn't found in a day or two.

A wrench saved him from a crash landing another time. The throttle control snapped off while the plane was in the air. Being an inspired mechanic from an early age, he thought that a vise grip wrench would hold the throttle if he had one aboard. He did, and it worked. From then on a wrench became an essential part of his tool kit.

Over the years, Wop's tool box filled up in direct proportion to his years of northern flying. It became a what's what of northern survival. Besides the extra bungee cords, tapes, and wires, he carried spark plugs, piston rings, sheet metal screws, nuts, bolts, lock washers, and lots of cotter pins. His inventory of emergency rations was equally extensive: safety pins, candles, a jacknife; chocolate, sugar, tea, rice, raisins, oatmeal; a Woods three-star sleeping bag, gun, fishing line, bandages. A tightly sealed case of wax-coated matches always got him a fire going even when everything else was wet. And the Bull Durham tobacco was always on board for almost every eventuality.

He continued to be relentless in his negotiations with Imperial Oil Company to make gasoline for airplane use. And finally they did.

As he told a radio interviewer in 1938:

*The pilot is the only link between the inhabitants of the north and the outside world, except of course the radio, and you would scarcely believe the sort of things which he is often asked to do. They treat him as a sort of fairy godfather. One chap asked us to bring rings for his marriage and bring the lady as well. One lady insisted she bring her canary along for the ride. We even carry ice cream beyond the Arctic Circle.*

# 1 0

# Tracking *the* Mad Trapper

**Dog teams hunting the mad trapper.**

Like many Canadians in the early days of 1932, Wop was following the Mounties' battle with the Mad Trapper in the daily newspaper. Like fewer Canadians, he could also tune it in on his crystal set and get the most up-to-date reports from the Aklavik radio station operated by the Royal Canadian Corps of Signals. As the Arctic outpost was also the northern RCMP headquarters, it would become the control centre for one of the largest manhunts in Canadian history. With all of it happening in his high Arctic country, Wop felt he had a personal stake in the story as it unfolded, so he paid close attention to it.

According to the news reports, it had started innocently enough. A man, who came to be called Albert Johnson, had floated down the Peel River from the general direction of the Yukon on a roughly built raft. He had tied up the raft about three miles above the

settlement of Fort McPherson in the Northwest Territories. There he had built himself a cabin, supposedly to do some trapping. Unlike most trappers in this remote area, however, Johnson seemed to prefer his own company, staying mysteriously apart from the residents and transients alike.

One day in December, 1931, one of the Indian trappers in the area found his traplines torn up and hung on trees. He complained about it to the RCMP and on the morning of December 30, Constable King and Special Constable Bernard set out from Aklavik on the 80-mile journey by dogsled to investigate the complaint. As they made their rounds of the cabins in the area for routine questioning, they eventually found their way to Albert Johnson's cabin. Smoke was coming from the chimney, usually an inviting signal for visitors ready for a warm rest.

This time, however, there was no response to the constables' greeting calls although they could hear sounds of someone inside. Heavy pounding on the door had no effect either. The message was clear: a search warrant would be needed. The men returned to Aklavik and got one, then, along with two other constables, they headed back to the cabin. This time they got a response they were not expecting: a volley of shots, one of which struck Constable King in the chest. They wasted no time in packing the wounded man into the dogsled and racing non-stop to the nearest doctor, back in Aklavik.

Hearing this report, Wop knew the pain of the wounded officer, bumping and hurtling through that snowswept wilderness for twenty hours in the wind-chilled, forty-below-zero temperature. He had seen many a dogteam at the end of such a run. There hadn't been much left of them. He knew that if he had been called he could have flown them back in fifteen minutes.

The next news report announced that two more patrols, made up of Inspector Eames, Constables McDowell and Millen, five special constables, and one guide had headed for the cabin on Rat River, this time fully prepared for battle. When they were greeted with the same response for two full days, they fired the dynamite they had brought with them.

As the smoke cleared they were surprised by yet another round of shots from a dazed but still enraged Johnson who remained within the protecting walls of his cabin. The patrols returned to Aklavik, regrouped, and five days later headed back. This time they found the cabin empty. The trapper had

vanished, leaving only footprints leading out and away from the cabin that had served him so well as a fortress. The hunt was on.

For much of the hunt, according to the daily reports, Johnson seemed to have the edge on his pursuers. He had the natural instincts of the hunted and was swift and sure in his own environment. The trails he left behind served only to put his hunters off his track, leading them invariably back to where they had started. Even the trappers and their teams who had joined the RCMP in their search had difficulty keeping track of their prey. Although they feared the unknown extent of his rage, they grew to respect his skills and endurance. As far as they knew, he had no bedroll, no tent, no stove, no provisions. Only the high-powered hunting rifle he had used against them at the cabin. His pursuers knew that he would never give away his hiding places by building fires large enough to cook any hare or ptarmigan he could snare. Yet he was obviously not starving for he was travelling quickly, continuing to keep well ahead of them in heavy snowshoes in temperatures that remained bitterly cold. He continued to do this for forty-eight days.

By the time the hunt reached the Richardson Mountains, virtually all of North America was tuned in to the Arctic drama. A growing number of Canadians and Americans would invest in radio sets just to get these daily reports from Aklavik. As they listened, the trapper became a killer. He shot and killed Constable Spike Millen. The RCMP was now under even more pressure to get this man before he disappeared forever. But just how they would do it was still beyond their reach.

The Mad Trapper Manhunt, 1932.
Top: The Bellanca aircraft at Aklavik; Centre: Wop May and Jack Bowen (mechanic); Bottom: L-R Sgt. Frank Riddell and S/S E.F. Hersey (Signals Corps) Jack Bowen (mechanic), Norman Hancock, Sgt. Major C. Neary, Jack Ethier (trapper), Wop May.

## Wop Joins the Hunt

Finally, they knew what was needed. A flying ace. Someone who could speed up their tracking, airlift their supplies from camp to camp. Someone who knew the river routes and mountain passes of the high Arctic. Someone who knew how to survive in the cold and barren northland.

On January 31, they contacted Canadian Airways for such a person and the Airways wired their man at Fort McMurray to take on the job.

Wop wasted no time in preparing for the mission. He and his mechanic, Jack Bowen, fine-tuned the Bellanca, packed the supplies which the company had flown up from Edmonton, and checked their emergency tool and ration kits. By the time Constable William Carter, the new recruit who had volunteered to replace Spike Millen, arrived from Edmonton, Wop was ready to board his plane.

Lifting off from Fort McMurray, Wop's thoughts were with the other part of the posse they would meet at the spot where Johnson had last been sighted. The ground posse had left Aklavik two days before, equipped with five heavily loaded sleds, seven men, and thirty-five dogs. Altogether, a lot of lives to stake on the pursuit of one man, and as the miles passed behind him, Wop's curiosity about the man increased. Who was he really? What had happened in his life to make him so desperate? What did he have to hide? Where had he come from and how had he learned such wilderness tactics? As much as the press had reported his moves, nothing had ever been reported about the man himself. The more Wop thought about this man the more he was anxious to meet up with him.

Remains of Johnson's cabin on the Rat River.

Other members of the posse were equally curious about the pilot as they watched him in action, especially on days when they had to carry out their operations in the frequent white-outs that covered the area. If it was difficult for them to see where the ground was ahead of them, how could the man in the air see it? How could he see to land? How could he see to fly in zero visibility?

On one such day, the sound of the 300-horsepower in action brought the others running toward the Bellanca. They shouted at Wop to turn off his engine, that a take-off was an impossibility. Sgt. Hersey, the army crackshooter of the posse, was to remember what he saw that day for the rest of his life. He had scanned the runway with his eyes, trying to hold himself steady against the howling wind. He couldn't see anything. Suddenly, in a brief break in the blowing snow, he saw something that froze his blood

in horror. He ran toward it. A mound of snow and ice had been built up by the wind as it hurried the snow through the pass. "Kind of like a mogul on a ski run" is the way he would describe it years later. Hersey realized immediately that there was no way Wop could see it from the cockpit. He ran towards the sound of the plane to try to stop Wop from taking off, but suddenly he was diving for cover as the Bellanca came hurtling out of the snow toward him, accelerating into a lift-off speed.

With the whole camp now watching for the inevitable disaster that was about to happen, they saw instead the plane lift one of its skis off the ground and step gracefully over the mound, missing not a skip of a beat or lessening its speed. They watched it carry on down the snow-covered strip until it was out of sight. As they listened to the plane rise and fly on somewhere above them they shook their heads in wonder at the man who had managed to do that, glad they were not tracking *him*.

Eventually, the hunt led them to the Yukon side of the mountains, where the tracks were slowing down through the deeper snow. It was now time to airlift the camp to LaPierre House as the RCMP closed in on their man. At last the day came when the tracks stopped altogether.

Making camp that night, the posse sensed that the end of their hunt was at hand. They had grown close during this ordeal, the constables, the army signal team, the pilot and his mechanic, and the trappers who had rallied to the call for a posse. The trappers, who had joined the hunt originally when it seemed everyone's traplines were in danger from this hostile trapper, became committed to his capture but were finally forced to return home to give their own traplines their overdue attention.

## Mad, or Cunning?

The biggest challenge of the hunt for the Army Signal Corps team of Hersey and

Quartermaster Sgt. Frank Riddell was in keeping their wireless set warm enough so they could keep in communication with Aklavik. They had wrapped the batteries up carefully when they packed them for the sled, but the set had still frozen in the forty-below temperature and did not respond. They knew they would have to find a way to keep those batteries warm next time, when they might not have a plane to provide them with a direct line of communication.

On this particular expedition such a radio connection had been necessary to meet the demands from the outside world for regular progress reports. For this pursuit had become headline news around the world. The principle character had even been given a name, the Mad Trapper. When the men involved in tracking him heard this, they questioned the media's assessment. This man they were pursuing was anything but mad. To them, he was a shrewd, organized, resolute, cold-blooded killer, who could perhaps end up killing all of them or making them crazy as he chased them around in circles.

## THE GIANTS

This Episode: Wilfred "Wop" May

McDayter and Drew, Calgary *Herald*, October 1965.

# THE GIANTS

This Episode: Wilfred "Wop" May

That night, they were silent and reflective, feeling the extent of their own tensions about this so-called Mad Trapper. His house had been blown up with him in it, but he hadn't died. He had tracked right past the huskies and they hadn't caught his scent. In all these many days of hunting him, none of the men had ever set eyes on him. Even the Indians feared him, seeing him more as an evil spirit than a man, and had refused to help in capturing him. Each man recognized how these days of hunting had depleted their energy and their spirits. They tried to make some sense out of why he had done what he had done, but they couldn't. They tried to keep the fear out of their minds of what he might still do to each and every one of them.

By morning, a fog had settled into the campsite. Wop sensed it even before he opened his eyes to it, and cursed his bad luck. Grounded!

Eames decided to head out with the ground crew and take the shortcut over to Eagle River where they had spotted the trapper the day before. They would leave trees down to guide the aerial team to them once the fog lifted.

Crack! Hersey with his strong team of seven Mackenzie River huskies was off with the dogsled part of the posse. Eames and Riddell followed them on snowshoes, and the others headed off on skis.

Wop looked up into the still thick air above him and wondered how long it would hold him to the ground, stifling his urge to let the Bellanca grope its way through the fog. In the meantime, he would make sure they were ready to go as soon as the fog lifted. Their checklists were gone over once, and then again. When the break came, he and his mechanic raced to the plane, eager to get this job finished. At long last they were flying toward Eagle River.

As they caught their first glimpse of the winding river, they could make out the black dots of the participants of this drama but could hear nothing above the noise of their engine. Wop flew lower and slower.

## Stopped at Last

There was a figure, dug into the deep snow of the river, his rifle aimed downstream. Wop and Jack started shooting some pictures of the battle taking place below them. They watched someone go down on his knees, hit.

Scene of the final shoot-out taken by Wop May and Jack Bowen. Johnson is the black dot in the centre of the river.

Then another. Then the others ran toward the second man down and aimed their guns at him, making his body jerk and jerk again until it lay still against the snow.

Very aware now who was who, Wop brought his machine down near Hersey and leaped out with Bowen close behind him. They picked up the sergeant off the snow and carried him into the plane. There they bound the gushing wound in his chest and made him as comfortable as they could for the ride ahead of them. With Bowen hanging on to Hersey, Wop started the plane. As the ground fell away below them, the storm took hold of the Bellanca, shaking it as if it were a kite cut loose of its string. Along with the wind came the snow, flinging itself against the windshield and whirling around the plane. With no way to see the ground below him, the mountains on either side, or the sky above, Wop realized he would have to feel his way out of this mountainous place, counting on his memory of the bends along the pass to know when and where and how to direct his plane.

An hour later they were in Aklavik. After getting Hersey to the hospital, Wop and Bowen waited, ready to make the seventeen-hundred mile flight to Edmonton with the wounded man if necessary. They didn't have long to wait for the doctor's report. The bullet that had brought Hersey down had ricocheted three times through his body and finally lodged just under the skin on his back, where it waited to be removed. As if to give them proof, the doctor showed them the bullet in his hand. With this settled, the flying team was on its way out the door, not even stopping to answer everyone's questions about the famous manhunt. They had a posse to pick up. And a body that had been taken by dogsled to LaPierre House and was waiting to be flown to Aklavik.

A shiver ran through Wop as he looked into the gaunt and gnarled face staring up at him from the bed of cold snow. The eyes and mouth were open in a frozen grimace as if the man were in the act of meeting the devil himself, knowing no more peace in death than he had in life. His bullet-riddled body was covered by tattered, worn wrappings, hardly adequate to withstand the winter cold let alone the ravaging forces of the northern Arctic. Wop half expected him to rise up, shake himself free of the snow and his pursuers, and continue on his way to wherever it was that he had been going before he had become the subject of such a chase.

The contents of the trapper's pockets gave them more cause to question the identity of this man. There was $2000 in cash, some of it American bills, as well as some gold fillings, and a pearl. Unlikely items for a trapper's gear. Was he a trapper at all? Was his name even Albert Johnson? What had he come for and where had he come from? What had been worth the life of one man and finally his own? None of these questions would ever be answered, for this man would keep his secrets forever.

They picked up the body and loaded it into the plane. The job was finally finished.

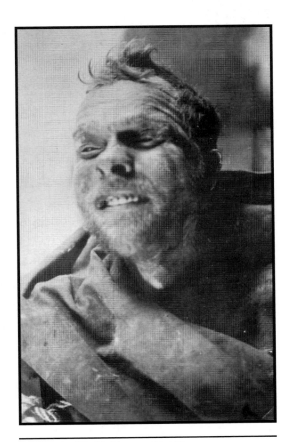

**Death mask of The Mad Trapper of Rat River.**

# 11
# Northern Flying Becomes *Big* Business

**Life as a bush pilot.**
**Archie McMullen and Wop May around the campfire.**

**M**issing bush pilots were always newsworthy, especially those who tended to attract exciting adventures. The north was full of unknown dangers for the men who were the last of the romantic adventurers in one of the last unopened frontiers. As one of the brotherhood, Wop May did his share of searching for missing bush pilots.

In the winter of 1934, Wop himself went missing.

His disappearance wasn't noticed for several days. Probably, if he hadn't been such a source of news for the media, it wouldn't have been noticed at all. He had planned this disappearance and planned it well. Only Vi knew about it, other than the two passengers and his mechanic, Rudy Heuss, who would go missing with him.

The four men were after a lost gold mine. Over the years, the search for this mine had attracted scores of prospectors. None had returned alive to tell about it. The death toll of treasure-seekers was such that the area became known as Dead Man's Valley. The number of headless skeletons found there prompted some to call it Headless Valley. The legend grew, that for a piece of gold from the valley you traded your head. Its location was only vaguely known as somewhere in the heart of the Nahanni Mountains.

Wop had spoken to many of the prospectors and trappers who had travelled in the north. As he listened to their stories of the lost gold mine, he became more and more interested in having his own turn at it. When he met an old priest who handed him the

Mealtime. Wop , left, with prospectors.

original map of the mine, he felt it was the hand of fate that he should consider going. And when two prospectors came to hire him to search for it, Wop made his decision.

Their destination a secret, Wop started his motor, excited at the idea of such an off-duty adventure, rubbing his good luck charms the whole way.

He landed the plane somewhat west of Dead Man's Valley, explaining to the others that it wouldn't do to disturb the sleeping spirits of the Nahannies. As they unloaded their gear, he instructed his mechanic to stay with the plane and guard it for their return. Then Wop and the two prospectors took to the ground until they came to the rocky cliffs of the hills. These they scaled, and from there descended into the misty valley, where they found a half-frozen creek running over a rocky bed. And there, just as the map had promised, were the remains of an ancient campsite exactly as they'd been left many years before.

That there was, in fact, hardly any treasure mattered very little, at least to the pilot. It was the excitement of the search that thrilled Wop. They had taken the route of a treasure map that led through a country of insurmountable odds, of unseen spirits, and they had found the site of the mine. It was a boy's dream come true. To the man, it was also the north revealing itself to the pilot who revered it. He had been entrusted with its secrets and been allowed safe passage. The glow from that would burn far brighter than any amount of gold they might have brought out from that lost gold mine.

Ten days later they turned up at Fort Simpson. By this time, Wop had been reported missing, had been searched for, and had been given up for dead. The sight of him now had the effect of the rising of a ghost. Wop enjoyed the sensation it created, one more party trick to add to his list. When everything calmed down he was able to find them all a good meal and get the news of their "rescue" back home.

## Wop and the Fandancer

The second time Wop was reported missing, he had nothing at all to do with it.

Camping at Cameron Bay. Wop on the left.

Although he had to spend a lot of time afterwards trying to convince his wife of that.

Like the rest of North America, Vi turned on the radio to the Sunday broadcasts of famed gossip columnist, Walter Winchell. This particular Sunday she was listening by herself, having waved good-bye once again to her sky-faring husband. As usual, he would be beyond any communication until return, whenever that might be.

Winchell's nasal news entered the room in its static buzz: "...famed Canadian bush pilot Wop May is reported missing somewhere between Winnipeg and The Pas, with his passenger being none other than that voluptuous fan dancer, Faye Baker. Watch out, Northern Canada. Watch out, Wop May. Could be in for a rough landing with this one...!"

"Missing" on a secret gold search was one thing. "Missing" with a beautiful fan dancer was quite another. And Vi's wait to get the truth was a long one. When Wop did finally return home he found his welcome lacked its usual warmth. As Vi told him about the news report, Wop was furious and immediately set about to uncover the truth. A public statement was issued that the misadventure had occurred to another bush pilot whose name also happened to be May and who did business in the northern Manitoba skies. This cleared up matters between Vi and Wop, and made Vi suggest that it was perhaps a suitable punishment for all

The joys of northern flying.
Top; The ice wasn't strong enough yet! Centre: Lift and repair. Bottom: Early snow. The Snye at the Fort McMurray float base (photo by George M. Douglas of Lakefield).

the practical jokes that Wop had inflicted on their friends over the years. Which in turn made Wop wonder if perhaps Vi had had something to do with the whole thing!

## The Fleet Grows

Wop's flying skills continued to make news throughout the remainder of his flying years in the north. One winter headline resulted from a takeoff from the Trout River along the MacKenzie River that broke one of the plane's skis. Not wanting to chance an emergency landing in an unfamiliar place with only one ski, Wop had decided to attempt a return to Trout River to repair it despite rough snow conditions. The event was witnessed by the three passengers on the aborted takeoff who had far more admiration for the pilot's one-ski landing than concern over their own safety.

By the mid-thirties, the northland was seen as Canada's richest storehouse of unlimited treasures. Gold, radium, water power, coal, gas, gypsum, lead, zinc, oil, copper, silver, mica, were all there for the taking, offering far more than trappers' dreams. And there, providing the force to mobilize all these riches, was the flight path of Canadian Airways Limited, the company that had purchased Commercial Airways two years after its first historic mail run. With its strategic location and proximity to Edmonton, and being on a rail and river steamer route, Fort

Top: Wop May's Junkers W-34 at the Northwest Minerals Camp on Lake Athabasca, Saskatchewan Centre: One method of carrying canoes on the Junkers with skis - Wop May at the top of the photo. Bottom: Carrying pontoons on the Junkers - Cooking Lake, Alberta.

One of Wop May's favorite aircraft on floats, CF-AKI, a Bellanca CH-300 Pacemaker.

The same aircraft on skis.

Unloading CF-ARI, Junkers W-34 , at Cooking Lake.

McMurray had become one of the largest commercial airbases in Canada. Trappers, fur traders, prospectors, miners, explorers, missionaries, priests, doctors, became regular passengers, along with His Majesty's Royal Mail, on Wop May's two-thousand-mile flights from Fort McMurray to Aklavik. As business grew, so did the size of planes, the speed at which they flew, and the number of the Canadian Airways fleet, which had increased to nine.

Wop was quick to give a lot of the credit for this progress to the President of Canadian Airways, James A. Richardson, whom he considered to be "The Father of Commercial Aviation in Canada."

In l934, Wop was promoted to captain. Two years later, he took over the northern operations as Superintendent of the McKenzie River District. When reporters cornered the busy flying superintendent in the fall of l938 and asked him what was new, he told them.

*We're flying Ford trucks in our flying boxcars. To explain more specifically, we have started carrying two hundred tons of freight for Consolidated Mining and Smelting Company from Goldfields to Tazin Lake for the hydro development there. They're loading machinery into the Junkers in chunks as big as four thousand pounds. Ford trucks are going in, half a truck at a time. In the north, gentlemen, we are ready and able to move anything, no matter how high we have to move them.*

Canadian Airways Aircraft Fleet at Fort McMurray, 1936. L-R: Fairchild FC-2W2, Junkers W-34, Junkers W-34, Fairchild 71C, Fairchild 82A.

# 12

# Another War, Another Call *to* Action

**Wop May with son Denny, Fort McMurray, 1936.**

During his aviation years, there was only one time when Wop May didn't fly high with the excitement of making a trip. It was May, l935. Fort McMurray on a beautiful spring day. Sky blue, wind calm, a perfect day for flying. All systems were go on the Bellanca. But the pilot was in an acute state of anxiety, and for the first time had no desire to be airborne. The mission was a highly personal one. Vi was pregnant and a pilot was needed to fly her to Edmonton to deliver their baby.

When it came to his personal life, Wop's superstitious nature played havoc with his skills and common sense as well as his proven ability to fly. No amount of juggling his worry stones or appealing to his wooden monkey, his usual good luck charm, could ease his fears this time. The birth of their first baby five years earlier still haunted him. The boy, Alexander Gerald, had been stillborn. Wop had been able to do nothing to help either mother or child. It had been a long time before the lights and the dance had returned to Vi's eyes and Wop couldn't bear to have that happen again. He had tried to find another pilot for the job, but Vi had refused to put herself into anyone else's hands. Wop was her man, her pilot, her lucky charm.

And so he was. Edmonton was safely reached, and Denny Reid was born on May l5, howling and kicking. There were no protests this time from the proud father who insisted on being the pilot for the trip home. He brought his family in with a perfect landing to the cheers of everyone in Fort McMurray who had gathered to welcome their arrival.

The May Family Christmas card, 1933.

Denny's sister Joyce, 1940.

Wop May was a public figure and a private man. On one occasion, when he was obliged to accept a speaking engagement, he rose awkwardly and made his way slowly to the speaker's lectern. The audience waited in excited anticipation for some heroic tales to be told by this famous adventurer. He finally

took a deep breath and spoke, hardly able to raise his eyes to look at them. It was a quiet and shy confession: "I would rather be flying under the most dangerous conditions than speaking here in front of you tonight." Although the spontaneous outburst of applause warmed him to his task, he was grateful when he could sit down and let others do the speaking.

His family was at the heart of his private life and the birth of his son was a major event. As was the death of his parents. When his father died in Edmonton in the fall of 1932, Wop was away in the far north, stranded by the freeze-up. Never able to take impossible for an answer, he searched for an alternative route in order to be with his family at this time. He located a pumper handcar on the Northern Alberta railway line, and proceeded to pump it by hand to the nearest train station in Lac La Biche, 150 miles away. There he caught the train and arrived in Edmonton in time for his father's funeral.

Wop, Denny & Vi May, Edmonton, 1939.

His mother's death seven years later would give him the same sense of loss and separation. It would be the first time his young son ever saw his father cry.

One day, when Denny was four, and the family had relocated in Edmonton, his father brought him home a sister, much to the concern of Vi who wanted to know more about the thin little girl than he had found her on an elevator. He finally admitted that she had been with a social worker heading for the adoption department. He simply followed them, signed the necessary papers, and brought her home so that Denny could have a sister. They called her Joyce.

And so the Mays became a family of four.

## A Chance to Teach Others

In the fall of 1936, Canadian Airways decided to expand and made some major moves. Punch Dickins, who had also gained a reputation as a bush pilot, was appointed Superintendent of Northern Operations. Wop, their Chief Pilot, was promoted to the position of Superintendent of Mackenzie District, with headquarters in Edmonton. The May family said farewell to Fort McMurray and headed for the city.

As it turned out, it was a very timely move for Wop. Very soon afterwards came the moment of truth with his sightless eye. The pain was now constant, affecting everything he did and felt. It became necessary for him to reveal the problem and undergo the surgery that could not save the eye but could relieve him of the pain. It could no longer be his and Vi's secret. But, like all other obstacles in their lives, it was to be faced

and overcome. There was a certain satisfaction for both of them that they had been able to keep the secret for fifteen years – it had been a long time to fly like an eagle with the sight of only one eye.

When Wop was told that he would have to get a new eye every year to accommodate the shrinking of the socket, he greeted the news with the full burst of his competitive spirit. It became a whole new sport for him to play with unsuspecting friends. One glass eye he took with him as a Christmas present to their friend Kay Dunlop in Calgary. His reward came in the form of a scream as Kay opened the beautifully gift-wrapped box and found an eye looking out at her.

However, with the declaration of World War Two, he felt once again the full despair of being a grounded flyer. He was no longer the twenty-year-old rookie who could move all obstacles to get into the skies to fight for his country, yet he still had the passion of that young man. With all of his heart and spirit he wanted to be able to fly again. The reality defeated him.

In the midst of this time of defeat came an unexpected call to arms, all the way from the top. Ottawa needed him to set up and manage a training school for pilots and navigators going overseas. At first he turned the call aside. He was unable to fly. He was a cripple, unfit for duty. Until he began to understand what it was they needed him to do: to teach others to carry out what he had always done so well. And for that, he didn't need whole vision. Like the true trooper he was, Wop rose to the occasion and agreed to do the job.

Staff at Air Observer School No.2, Edmonton, 1944. Back row L-R: Dr. Eliott Cohen (Doctor), Wop May (Manager), Jack Lickert (Faculties Superintendent), Front row L-R: Pat Brooks (Secretary), Leonard Sawle (Assistant Manager?), Mary Hammond (Secretary).

Canada's part in the British Commonwealth Air Training Plan was to prepare pilots, navigators and observers for the war. When it got underway, there would be ten training bases across Canada, operating over 4000 aircraft and graduating over 2200 combat crews per month, from every country in the Commonwealth.

The prototype, Observer School No. l, had been formed in Malton, so Wop's first job was to take a look at the Malton operation to see how it worked. Then he headed back to Edmonton to set up Observer School No. 2, eager to teach others what they would need to know to survive and win the war in the air.

Students were introduced to the RCAF at an initial four-week training course. They then spent twelve weeks flying over Edmonton in their yellow training Avro Ansons, at any time of day or night, first of all beside their

instructor and then on their own. They were then considered ready for six weeks of bombing and gunnery school. The program ended with a session in celestial navigation. The successful graduates received their flying colours and their ticket overseas when all this was completed.

Because they were "Wop's boys", the students were always invited home. There Vi put them to work shovelling snow or digging in the garden. She invariably challenged them to beat her at squaw wrestling and, of course, invited them to stay for dinner. Denny was old enough by this time to get in on the act and knew an audience when he saw one. Out would come the scrapbooks of newspaper clippings and photographs, as well as the treasures from the trunk, and Wop would be forced to tell the tales behind them all. While his experiences gave the young men something high to aim for, Wop knew only too well the reality of the place where they were heading, the reality of war, where they would be lucky to survive once they were in the air with artillery all around them. Despite all the knowledge and skill they took with them from this training, many of them would get killed and there was nothing he could do about it. It was a reality that kept Wop in a daily state of inner conflict, for these were his boys.

## Search, Jump, and Rescue

It was during this time that Wop saw a chance to save some lives on the home front as well and he took it. These were to become his American boys. They were flying through Wop's beloved north country to ferry their aircraft into Russia, but they were getting lost in the process. There was no successful way of keeping track of their whereabouts, and when they went down in that northern wilderness there was no way of finding them. Wop was often asked to go along on these search and rescue missions to help locate the downed plane but even if the plane was found, it was too late to save anyone on board. The frigid temperatures would claim the ones who had managed to survive the initial crash if help did not come in time.

Many years later Vi still recalled the night that Wop came up with the answer to this rescue problem. As usual, he had confided his fears to her. Sharing them eased the weight from his own shoulders and he valued her input. He had just returned from yet another unsuccessful rescue mission where some of the frozen crew could have been saved if they had been able to get to them faster. Vi could see that he was taking this failure personally. They began to brainstorm the possible alternatives to carrying out a rescue from a plane that was unable to land. It wasn't long before Wop could see the picture clearly enough to see a parachute in it, with food, medical supplies, a doctor even. Then he stopped, flushed with excitement and burst out laughing. That's when he told her about one of his new boys who'd been bugging him lately to let him jump. He'd tried to get rid of the boy. But, as he confessed to Vi, there was something about this kid that reminded him of the way he himself had been to his C.O. back when he had been so eager to fly. Vi wasn't surprised to get a good-bye hug that night as Wop raced back to the airbase to get a young and eager jumper out of bed and start his search and rescue operation.

While Wop watched from the ground with Denny at his side, the first jumper landed on the American Officers' Mess. Another one actually landed on the runway, but flat-footed. One young jumper landed on the wing of an airplane and fell right through. So up they went again. And again they managed to miss their scheduled landing places. When Wop admonished the young enthusiast who had been the one to bug him into jumping in the first place, he was quickly, and politely, reminded that their jumping was okay, it was just the landing they hadn't figured out yet.

Then an American Air Force Officer who had been observing the procedures offered a proposition that Wop readily accepted. He

Brigadier-General Dale Gaffney, representing the United States of America, presents the Medal of Freedom, with Bronze Palm to W.R. Wop May. Edmonton, February 24, 1947.

invited Wop to send his boys down to Missoula, Montana, where they were training smoke jumpers. They had room for these para-rookies and would be happy to be part of Wop's rescue program. As the officer reminded Wop, they had a vested interest in the training of his rescue teams. After all, it would be American troops, among others, who would benefit from the rescue efforts.

With his first parachute crew off learning how to jump, Wop set himself to the task of designing the rescue part of the program, drawing on his own survival experience. His crews would have to learn how to save the lives of those they were rescuing, as well as their own lives, no matter what situation or what conditions they would encounter.

At the end of the war when the Air Observer Schools were no longer needed, they were closed down. But the RCAF kept the well established search and rescue unit in operation, recognizing it as an essential part of their North West Air Command.

In 1947, the American Government honoured Wop with the American Medal of Freedom. At the presentation ceremony, the citation was read aloud:

> He voluntarily loaned the personnel and the facilities of his school to ensure the delivery of aircraft to the Aleutians and Alaska without delay. He conceived the idea of aerial rescue crews for rescue of flyers in the bush area and after developing a trained parachute squad he furnished a rescue service indiscriminately to Americans and Canadians, thus saving the lives of many of our flyers. In so doing he fulfilled the highest tradition of the Dominion of Canada.

As Wop stopped briefly for pictures and questions from the press following the presentation, a reporter asked him what it was like to jump.

"Jump!? Me jump? Are you crazy! A guy could get killed jumping out of a plane."

When the laughter subsided, he said in a more serious tone: "I was never the one to jump. I give all the credit to the people who did the jumping in the north. It is to them the northern flyers owe their lives."

## THE GIANTS

This Episode: Wilfred "Wop" May

McDayter and Drew, Calgary *Herald*, October 1965.

# 13

# Family Matters

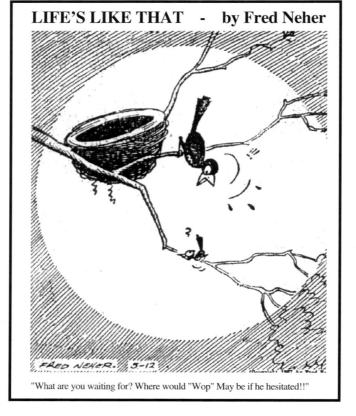

**LIFE'S LIKE THAT - by Fred Neher**

FRED NEHER. 5-12

"What are you waiting for? Where would "Wop" May be if he hesitated!!"

In the spring of 1941, Wop suffered a heart attack. Despite his many encounters with death, this was the first time he felt the impact of his own mortality. It landed him in the hospital and confined him to a wheelchair. It grounded him with a lifestyle that his spirit was totally unprepared for and that his body had no way of fighting. His doctor didn't mince words or give him any options. He was to lose weight, stop smoking, and quit drinking. There was to be no excitement, no working, and no walking. The doctor then introduced him to the vehicle he would be using until further notice and presented the person who would be in charge of making sure he carried out those orders. Vi knew it would likely be the most challenging hurdle of her life, but she also knew she wouldn't want anyone else to do it. As Wop conceded to the inevitable, he let them help him into the wheelchair and allowed his "new C.O." to take him home.

For the next few months, Wop's body got its first rest in forty-five years. Although he was plagued with bouts of depression, his restless spirit found some degree of peace during this confinement. His family enjoyed the luxury of having him where they could find him. In some ways, they got to know him for the first time, and they grew close. It was a closeness that he would nurture over the next few years, and in so doing, he learned to reveal himself to them.

When the day was done and the strains of Rhapsody in Blue floated through the house, Vi would go to the tobacco cupboard, load up with the supplies and join him. It became a ritual with them, each of them rolling a cigarette, then together enjoying the silence of their companionship and the sharing of past experiences and future visions.

When he was finally declared well enough by his doctor to head back to work Wop made room in his busy schedule for special times with his family. Whenever he was away from home, he would be in daily touch by letter or postcard. Sometimes there would be a practical message: "Vi. Forgot to tell you I think there's a leak in the rear end of the car as I noticed some spots on the garage floor. Better take it in." Sometimes there was a poem to the woman he loved: "Vi Dear. Last night I picked up a book and read a poem that just seemed to hit me right, so I just thought I'd send it along.

> One looks behind him to some vanished time, and says "Ah I was happy then, alack!
> I did not know it was my life's best prime – Oh, if I could go back!
> Another looks, with eager eyes aglow, to some glad day of joy that yet will dawn, and sighs, I shall be happy then, I know, Oh, let me hurry on!
> But I – I look out on my fair today,

> I clasp it close, and kiss its radiant brow.
> Here with the perfect present let me stay for I am happy now!

"That's me Vi old dear. I am happy and it's all your fault you see. Well, here's wishing you a very Merry Christmas Vi, and I hope you like it. Lovingly Wopsie."

Sometimes it was a response to a son's letter:

> Little fellow.
> Was sure swell to get your letter. Was surprised to hear you were a bad boy. That's that other Boy that comes around once in a while, eh? Am going fishing now. Wish you were here too.

## Lessons in Adventure

When he was home he became intent on teaching Denny and Joyce how to survive in the wilds. His first lessons were in the bush near their Edmonton home in the winter and in the rain. There he would show them how to find dry tinder even amongst the dripping wet bush.

"You've got one match to get that started," Denny would be told. And if that didn't do it, another campfire would be built and another single match doled out to light it. "It could very well save your life one day," Wop would say, giving his son a proud hug as the first flame took hold in the pouring rain.

When Denny reached twelve, it was declared time to go camping for real. Time also for his sister to be initiated. As Vi waved them off on the July morning in their DC-3, she knew that the children were about to get the lesson of their lives. It became Denny's initiation to the north, an event that would keep him coming back for more for the rest of his life. They left the passenger plane at Yellowknife and hopped aboard Ernie Boffa's Norseman to get to Wop's favourite fishing hole at Gunbarrel Inlet on Great Bear Lake.

The children, excited with the plane ride, did not greet the landing place with the same enthusiasm. It was bare rock and scant bush. Nothing to find, nowhere to go, and water too cold to play in. Their complaints had no effect upon their father who was determined that they would learn to survive and to do it in comfort and style. Joyce was put in charge of gathering the moss for a soft bed. Denny was the fire-builder, cautioned to make it small so he could get close enough without burning himself when it was time for him to cook the fish for dinner. Catching the fish was everybody's favourite job. Come bedtime, the children loved to listen to their father's stories about the strange things he had seen and heard in his northern flying adventures.

Although they enjoyed most of their father's choice of other edibles, such as eggs, milk, lemons, rice, raisins, chocolate, and canned goods, and ate hungrily, they refused to try his particular way of enjoying them. Joyce would make a face as she watched him break off the tops of his eggs and suck out the raw insides. Denny was astonished to watch his father blend milk with lemon juice and gulp the soured mixture. Wop enjoyed their reaction and would smack his lips at such northern delicacies. But the children's attention even to their father's performances

had a limit, and the sound of the returning Norseman was greeted with enthusiasm.

The next stop on this campout was Coppermine, where Wop dropped off his young charges for a few days while he carried on to Campbridge Bay to take care of some business. As the Norseman took off, he caught a glimpse of his young son running ahead of RCMP Constable Martin Donnan, towards the barracks where he would stay until his dad's return. Joyce had already been whisked off to the Anglican manse by Canon Webster and his wife, and there, he was sure, she would be properly spoiled.

Both children had a fine time but they had missed him and greeted his return excitedly. He had been right about Joyce. She had been spoiled by everyone. But Denny's visit had filled his head with wonderment. Wop was now the listener and Denny the teller of tales — about how the fish were dried, and how Donnan had taken him out on a boat to an ice flow and he had found out where the prisoners stayed which was guess where? right behind where he slept! and guess who's there right now? the cook! and guess why he's there? he's killed a man!

As Wop watched the blazing eyes of his son, he realized that the trip hadn't shown him how to survive, but it had injected him with a fever for the north. He would settle for that.

## More Family Flying Trips

Their return home was made via Port Radium. As the Norseman started up off Great Bear Lake on the last lap of the journey, it became clear that there wasn't enough wind to lift off. Wop asked Ernie to let him have a go at it. Ernie was grateful to hand over the controls. Like most bush pilots he was in awe of the legend of Wop May and had been a little nervous to be his pilot on this trip. So he was glad to sit back and learn from the legend himself.

One, two, three, four circles of the plane in the water, creating the much-needed waves on the still, windless lake. Then out of the last circle, Wop made a sharp turn back into those waves and, as if in obedience to the master, the Norseman sailed off the water and rose into the air. It had been a long time since Wop had been at the controls. It felt good. He thanked Ernie as he handed the plane back. To Ernie's unspoken question, Wop simply called it a little trick he'd learned along the way.

Wop would feed Denny's new excitement for the north with other trips. One such trip was to take a parrot to Yellowknife. A friend had told Wop that the bird needed a home because it had bitten off the owner's finger and wasn't welcomed back into the family. Wop decided it would make a great party stopper, and his family needn't know what the bird did to fingers. So the raven-sized Polly came home to terrify, intimidate, and amuse the May family for two years.

When it refused to perform at parties with anything more than "I'm going to run away" and a string of unacceptable expletives, it was time to find the parrot another home. Somewhere far enough away that the bird couldn't find her way back to their house. Why not in Yellowknife? Wop's friend Vic Ingram, who had needed a ride out from Aklavik on Wop's plane back in 1933 for a leg amputation, now owned a hotel in Yellowknife. Vic was easy to convince that a large parrot would attract more customers to his hotel. But getting the bird there proved to be a major challenge.

Polly was securely packed in seven cardboard boxes for the trip and carefully placed on board the DC-3 in the curtained-off luggage space between the passengers and the pilot. It did not take too many air miles before Polly had eaten her way through all seven layers of cardboard and was free. Wop was ordered to restrain his parrot. The deed was finally done with all fingers intact and only a few missing feathers. Wop sat on the box the rest of the way, with Denny on duty to watch for any signs of an escaping parrot. Polly and her entourage arrived safely in Yellowknife, where she became the main attraction of the hotel until the place burned down some years later.

In his son's thirteenth year, Wop planned another trip with him. On his calendar, if not on Denny's, it was time for a young man to learn to be a hunter. For Wop, it was an annual hunting trek to guarantee the family a year's supply of caribou. It had often been the only meat on the table during the long, lean winter months. For Denny, however, it would become a one-time-only ordeal.

Because Wop knew the winter migratory trail of the caribou, it didn't take him long to find them and give the pilot instructions on where to land. It was a large herd, so there would be lots of meat for everyone on this hunting expedition. Denny's excitement did not match that of his father... he was cold and he knew he was not the hunter that his dad wanted him to be. When the plane landed he pressed his nose against the window, transfixed at the sight of the magnificent creatures standing so proudly there in the snow.

Wop, knowing the animals would become nervous at their arrival and likely run, had instructed his son to be ready to move as soon as the plane landed. He had already taught Denny how to hold a rifle and aim it for a good clean kill for the time when Denny would be old enough to have his own gun. For now, Denny was only to watch and learn. As the hunters piled out of the plane, the clean kills began. Before very long the white snow was covered with blood and bleeding carcasses. Only a few of the herd had escaped.

Preoccupied with the kill and the cleaning of each beast, Wop hadn't noticed that his son hadn't left the side of the plane. When he finally saw him, Denny was shivering, his whole body was in spasm. Wop hurried over and brought the boy to the animal he had

been cleaning. He held open the steaming belly that he had just slit and told Denny to put his hands inside to warm them.

Denny looked in horror at the sight in front of him, then turned and ran back to the plane, clutching his own stomach to try to keep from throwing up.

# 14
# Final Stages *of* Departure

Wop May opens Canadian Pacific Airlines operations in the Far East and the South Pacific, 1949-1950.

**W**ith the closing of Air Observer School No. 2 at the end of the war, Wop had returned to his former post as Superintendent of the Mackenzie River District. But by now Canadian Airways had become Canadian Pacific Airlines (CPA) as the world moved into global aviation. For the next five years he put his energy and knowledge to work as Director of Northern Development for CPA, opening up official air bases all over the north for Norseman, DC-3, and Canso flying.

Already well known by most of the northern population, Wop had no difficulty in negotiating for a CPA office in the town. Then he would wire the operating personnel and move in the agents to handle the business. In this way, the northern operations expanded to include Yellowknife, Coppermine, Whitehorse, Dawson City, Fairbanks, and Fort Smith.

In 1949, he was transferred to Vancouver as Director of Development for CPA. After he had established an airport for Northern British Columbia at Sandspit, near Prince Rupert, he turned his attention across the Pacific and proceeded to negotiate with the governments of other countries to make CPA part of an international flying route. Canadians soon found themselves able to fly to Honolulu, Fiji, Sydney, Auckland, Hong Kong, Tokyo, Bangkok, Singapore, and Shanghai for the first time.

No one was as excited to be on an international flight as the trail-blazing Director of Development himself. No one brought home more souvenirs or was welcomed back with more excitement than

Wop, who had exotic gifts for everyone from far-off lands across the sea.

In 1951 CPA had successfully bid on a contract with the RCAF and the RCN to recover crashed aircraft, repair them, and test-fly them for service again. Wop was asked to head up the new operation, to be known as CPA (Repairs) Limited, and the family moved to Calgary.

This time the family made their home right on the airbase to accommodate a demanding job that called Wop into duty at all hours of the day and night. It was to be his final contribution to the company and to Canadian aviation.

One day, while completing a report at his desk, Wop noticed with surprise that it was spring. Almost a year since he had started bringing in the military aircraft and restoring them. He felt good about what he had been able to accomplish in such a short time and about the plans for enlarging the operation.

Suddenly he winced. Pain. He clutched his chest and then commanded himself to ease back in his chair and relax. Gradually the pain subsided, leaving him with a dreadful weariness. He recalled Vi's suggestion that he take some time off. He decided to do just that.

Vi would remember the pain in his voice as he phoned her that day to tell her he wanted to take Denny on a camping trip to Timpanogos Cave National Monument at American Fork in Utah. She winced at his plans to do some hiking near Salt Lake City, but said nothing. And then she listened to what she knew was his farewell to her. It was a poem he had found.

"I think I'm going to keep this one real close," he told her, "because it makes me think of you. It goes like this..." and he read her the poem:

I love you not only for what you are
but for what I am when I am with you.
I love you not for what you have made of yourself
but for what you are making of me.
I love you for the part of me that you bring out.
I love you because you are helping me
to make out of the lumber of my life
not a tavern, but a temple.
Out of the works of every day,
not a reproach but a song.
I love you because you have done more than any creed could have done to make me good
and more than any fate could have done to make me happy.
You have done it without a scold, without a reproach, without a sign of anything, but Love.

They would find the poem, carefully folded in his pocket, heading up that hill to Timpanogos Cave.

# Epilogue

Last photo of Wop May, taken by his son on the trail to Timpanogos Cave, American Fork, Utah just minutes before he died. June 21, 1952.

We were 35,000 feet in the air, smoothly gliding over the Sierra Nevada. The captain of the 737 had invited us to visit him in his cabin.

"We get bored up here with nothing to do on a long flight."

"Bored!?" I burst out, having been immersed in the world of Wop May whose flying moments were anything but. "How can you be bored when you're flying a plane?"

"Well, actually, we have very little to do with it once we're in the air. This tells us what to do and how we're to do it." He held up a computer print-out and showed it to me. "And these do the rest." He pointed to the dials with arrows and numbers in front of him and above him.

"Wop would never have believed this," I mused aloud.

"Wop? Did you say Wop?" asked the captain. "As in Wop May?"

"Why yes. Did you know him?"

"Well, I feel I knew him. But really I only knew of him. I flew the Arctic before I got into these routes. We all knew of Wop May. We flew because of Wop May. We used his maps, his routes, his methods of northern survival. He showed us how to do it. Wop May. He could fly blind-folded with his hands tied behind his back. Why, do you know how one time his throttle broke, in mid-air..." The stories started. Having studied the man and researched the facts, I was fascinated now to hear the stories.

Finally, bringing himself back to the reality around him, the captain said, "And look at us now. The age of high tech. We know the exact second we will touch down, it's all programmed. Wop would have understood all that for he helped us get here. But you know something? I don't think he would have been happy flying this way. He flew by the seat of his pants, lucky to arrive at all, happy if he beat his own record of speed and time."

The co-pilot, a younger man, had listened intently to the stories, his imagination obviously aroused. "Sounds like he left us quite a legacy. I can hardly wait to read the book."

– Sheila Reid

# Chronology

| | | |
|---|---|---|
| **1896** | | Wilfrid Reid May born March 20, Carberry, Manitoba. Named after Liberal Prime Minister Sir Wilfrid Laurier. |
| **1902** | | May family moved from Carberry to Edmonton. |
| **1903** | | Wilfrid started school, Mackay Ave. School, Edmonton. |
| **1908** | | Attended Victoria Composite School, Edmonton. |
| **1914** | | Attended Western Canada College in Calgary. |
| **1916** | | Enlisted in the 202nd "City of Edmonton" Sportsman Battalion of the Canadian Infantry in January, and by July 1917 held the rank of Sergeant serving as a gunnery instructor. |
| **1917** | | Granted a Commission in July in the Royal Flying Corps. Began flying training in October at the Royal Flying Corps School of Instruction, Acton, England. |
| **1917** | | First solo flight, November 17—total previous flying time 3 hours, 29 minutes. |
| **1918** | **April 9** | Reported to 209 (9th Naval) Squadron, RFC, France, flying Sopwith Camels. |
| **1918** | **April 20** | First combat mission. |
| **1918** | **April 21** | S/L Roy Brown credited with shooting down The Red Baron, Manfred von Richtofen, who had pursued Wop May across the Allied lines. Australian gunners also credited with the shooting—evidence suggests they delivered the fatal bullet. |
| **1918** | **Sept. 12** | Awarded the Distinguished Flying Cross. |
| **1919** | **July 7** | Issued Aero Club of Canada Pilot's Licence #7 and Air Mechanic Licence #1. |
| **1919** | **July 12** | During Fair Week flew Edmonton mayor Joe Clarke under the High Level Bridge so he could throw the first ball of the season at Diamond Baseball Park. |
| **1919** | | Formed, with his brother Court May, May Airplanes Limited in Edmonton, flying the Curtis Jenny the "City of Edmonton." |
| **1921** | | In January he flew the Junkers-Larsen JL-6 monoplane from New York to Edmonton for Imperial Oil Ltd. |
| **1921** | **May 7** | Became Chief Pilot for Great North Service. |
| **1924** | **March 12** | L.H. Adair's Curtiss Jenny left San Diego for Seattle, flown by U.S. aviator N.B. Mayner. Hugh Hill flew it to the Canadian border, then Wop May flew it on to Grande Prairie. |
| **1924** | **Nov. 20** | Married Violet A. Bode in Edmonton. |
| **1924** | | Worked for National Cash Register as a mechanic. A steel splinter entered his eye, leading to reduced eyesight and eventually to the loss of his eye in 1936. |
| **1927** | | Edmonton Aero Club organized. Wop May was the president and chief instructor. |
| **1928** | **Nov. 24** | With his companion Blake Dagg, set an altitude record for Northern Alberta of 10,000 feet. |
| **1929** | **Jan. 2** | With Vic Horner, flew serum to Fort Vermilion to help prevent diphtheria epidemic. They experienced temperatures of -30°F. Their plane was an Avro Avian with wheels. They returned as heroes to a welcoming crowd of 10,000. |
| **1929** | **Feb. 5** | Flew a nurse to Westlock with diphtheria antitoxin. |
| **1929** | **Feb. 20** | Calgary Kinsmen Club honoured Wop May and Vic Horner at a banquet at the Paliser Hotel. |
| **1929** | **May 10** | Edmonton honours May and Horner with a banquet, parade, and presentation of gold watches. |
| **1929** | **May 25** | Wop set speed record to Winnipeg: 6 hours, 48 minutes. In a borrowed plane, he was 2nd in Aerobatics at air show. |

| 1929 May 29 | Forced down in Lockheed Vega at Glamis, Saskatchewan. |
|---|---|
| 1929 July 10 | Flew Dr. Harold Hamman to Carcajou to treat Mrs. Frank Jackson; on July 28 flew to Keg River to bring her, her infant son and Dr. Hamman to Edmonton. |
| 1929 Aug. 17 | Flew to Vegreville to bring out patient with broken leg. |
| 1929 Oct. 25 | Set speed record to Calgary; 1 hour 30 minutes in a Bellanca. Passengers were Premier Brownlee, Hon. O.L. McPherson, W.G. Stedman, Harvey Mills & Audrey Michaels. |
| 1929 Dec. 1 | First air mail flight to Aklavik, NWT from Edmonton, 30 days round trip. |
| 1930 Feb. 8 | Avro Avian sold to Rutledge Air Service, Saskatoon. |
| 1930 May 1 | Wop was awarded the McKee Trophy for 1929. |
| 1930 July 23 | First air mail to Fort McMurray, Alberta. |
| 1931 May 8 | Commercial Airways taken over by Canadian Airways Limited. |
| 1932 Feb. 3 | Wop flew to Aklavik to aid in the hunt for the Mad Trapper, Albert Johnson. He finally spotted Johnson on the Porcupine River in the Yukon. This was the first time an aircraft was used in a manhunt by the RCMP. |
| 1932 Feb. 17 | Albert Johnson was killed by an RCMP posse and his body was flown back to Aklavik the following day. |
| 1932 Sept. 12 | Wop flew from Great Bear Lake, NWT to Fort McMurray in 5 hours and 57 minutes. |
| 1933 Jan. 31 | He located the wreckage of the aircraft in which Paul Calder and W.B. Nadin died near Grouard Lake, 90 miles south of Cameron Bay, NWT. |
| 1933 Dec. 2 | Wop brought Vic Ingram out from Aklavik to Edmonton for leg amputation. |
| 1934 Jan. 25 | After he had been missing for a week due to a broken plane ski at Trout River, NWT, Wop reported in at Fort Simpson. |
| 1934 Feb. 14 | He flew 821 miles in one day, from Cameron Bay to Fort McMurray. |
| 1935 Jan. 1 | Wop May was awarded the Order of the British Empire. |
| 1935 May 15 | Wop's son Denny Reid May was born in Edmonton. |
| 1935 June 12 | He flew his wife Vi and their new baby back to Fort McMurray in a Bellanca aircraft. |
| 1935 Dec. 12 | His aircraft went through the ice while landing on the Slave River at Fort Chipewyan, Alberta. |
| 1936 Sept. | Wop flew Governor General, Lord Tweedsmuir (John Buchan) on a tour of the Northwest Territories. |
| 1936 Sept. | The operation was performed to remove his eye. Wop lost his pilot's licence as a result. |
| 1940 Aug. | Wop was appointed manager of #2 Air Observer School (British Commonwealth Air Training Plan), Edmonton. |
| 1944 July 8 | Wop May and Freddy McCall have a historic meeting after 26 years. |
| 1947 Feb. 24 | United States Brigadier General Dale Gafney presents the Medal of Freedom with Bronze Palm to Wop May in recognition of his role in the formation of the Para-Rescue School in Edmonton, which resulted in saving the lives of many American Airmen flying the "Polar Staging Route" during WW II. |
| 1947 Feb. 24 | Wop was appointed Director of Northern Development for Canadian Pacific Airlines (CPA) - which opened bases throughout the NWT, Yukon and Alaska. |
| 1949 July 1 | He was appointed Director of Development for Canadian Pacific Airlines (CPA), and opened bases in Hawaii, Tokyo, Singapore, Shanghai, Bankok, Nandi, Auckland and Sidney. |
| 1951 July 1 | Appointed manager of CPA (Repairs) Ltd in Calgary. |
| 1952 June 21 | Wop May died in Provo Utah, while on a hiking trip with his son Denny. His body was flown back to Edmonton for burial. |
| 1973 Dec. 31 | Wop May was inducted into Canada's Aviation Hall of Fame in Edmonton. Vi May accepted the honours. |

# Index